Amazing Amphibians

OTHER TITLES IN THE
YOUNG NATURALISTS SERIES

*Awesome Snake Science! 40 Activities
for Learning About Snakes*

*Birdology: 30 Activities and Observations
for Exploring the World of Birds*

*Insectigations: 40 Hands-on Activities
to Explore the Insect World*

*Plantology: 30 Activities and Observations
for Exploring the World of Plants*

*Treecology: 30 Activities and Observations for
Exploring the World of Trees and Forests*

**Young
NATURALISTS**

Amazing Amphibians

30 Activities and Observations for Exploring Frogs, Toads, Salamanders, and More

Lisa J. Amstutz

CHICAGO REVIEW PRESS

Published by Chicago Review Press Incorporated
814 North Franklin Street
Chicago, Illinois 60610
ISBN 978-1-64160-072-9

Library of Congress Cataloging-in-Publication Data
Names: Amstutz, Lisa J., author.
Title: Amazing amphibians : 30 activities and observations for exploring
    frogs, toads, salamanders, and more / Lisa J. Amstutz.
Description: Chicago, Illinois : Chicago Review Press, [2020] | Series:
    Young naturalists | Includes bibliographical references and index. |
    Audience: Ages 7-9 | Audience: Grades 2-3 | Summary: "Amazing
    Amphibians explores the major amphibian groups-frogs, salamanders and
    caecilians-including their anatomy, behavior and conservation needs"—
    Provided by publisher.
Identifiers: LCCN 2019032671 (print) | LCCN 2019032672 (ebook) | ISBN
    9781641600729 (paperback) | ISBN 9781641600736 (pdf) | ISBN
    9781641600743 (mobi) | ISBN 9781641600750 (epub)
Subjects: LCSH: Amphibians—Juvenile literature.
Classification: LCC QL644.2 .A4748 2020 (print) | LCC QL644.2 (ebook) |
    DDC 597.8—dc23
LC record available at https://lccn.loc.gov/2019032671
LC ebook record available at https://lccn.loc.gov/2019032672

Cover and interior design: Sarah Olson
Cover photos: frog eggs, Geoff Gallice/Wikimedia Commons;
blue frog, suju/Pixabay; salamader, Chris Mattison/Nature Picture
Library; smooth newt nymph, Martin Pelanek/Shutterstock.com.
Interior illustrations: Jim Spence

Printed in the United States of America
5 4 3 2 1

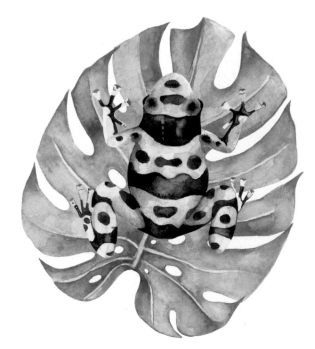

This book is dedicated to all the small and underappreciated creatures of the world and to all the biologists, conservationists, and citizen scientists working to protect them. Their work truly makes a difference!

Brum/Shutterstock.com

Contents

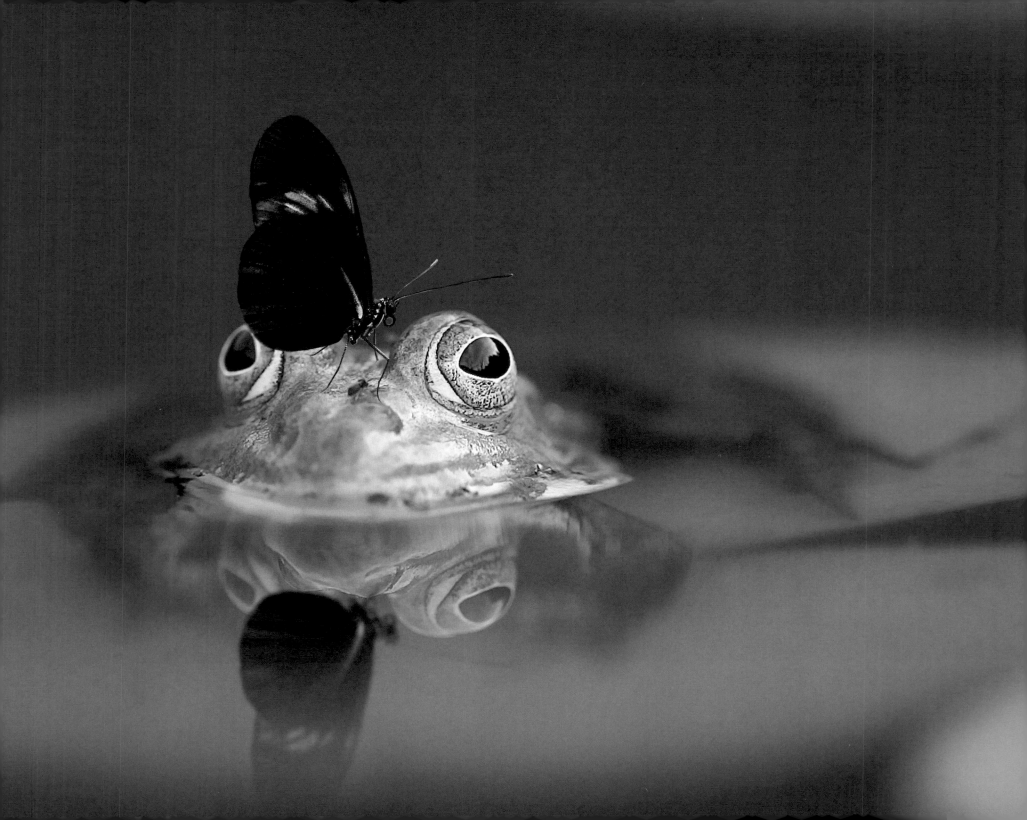

Acknowledgments

I am grateful for the love and support of my husband and kids, who continually inspire me and good-naturedly put up with my long hours at the computer. I am also grateful to my parents, who taught me to love nature and kept me well supplied with books throughout my childhood.

Huge thanks to Matt Neff for sharing his amphibian expertise. And last but certainly not least, many thanks to Victoria Selvaggio for her ongoing support and friendship and to editors Lisa Reardon and Jerome Pohlen, who believed in this book and brought it to life.

FrankWinkler/Pixabay

Introduction

Amphibians live almost everywhere, but they can be hard to find for much of the year. In spring, however, frogs and toads fill the night air with their songs and lay masses of eggs in and around ponds and streams, as do salamanders. If you provide a **habitat** for them, you may be able to attract amphibian visitors to your yard.

Amphibians are not only fascinating and beautiful; they are also beneficial to humans in many ways. One big benefit they provide is that they eat pests of all kinds. They are also eaten by larger animals. Amphibians are a vital link in the food webs of many different ecosystems.

There is still much to learn about many of these secretive creatures, especially the caecilians, which spend most of their lives underground. New amphibian species are being discovered every day, and scientists can now use high-tech tools such as DNA sequencing to figure out where they fit into the amphibian family tree. In 2003, scientists even discovered a whole new family of frogs in the mountains of southern India. Only one species in this family has been identified so far. This is an exciting time to be a herpetologist!

The last few decades, however, have brought new challenges. Amphibian populations have shrunk dramatically, and some species have become endangered or extinct. Many factors are involved in this decline, including diseases, pollution, and habitat loss. Scientists and conservationists are working hard to figure out what is causing this decline and to protect endangered species before it is too late.

In this book, you'll learn lots of fascinating facts about amphibians and create an explorer's notebook to keep track of your findings. Each chapter includes fun activities to help you learn more. It can be difficult to identify amphibian species, and there are too many to include them all in this book. But you will learn to study them carefully and observe their differences.

IMPORTANT!

Amphibians are fragile creatures due to their sensitive skin, and **it is best not to pick them up**. If you do, be very careful when handling them, as some produce toxins that can make you ill. Wash your hands carefully after touching any amphibian.

It's fun to go looking for amphibians, but **always tell an adult where you are going**. You don't need to go far—you can probably find amphibians in your local park or even your backyard.

Gary Wells/ Flickr

1

What Is an Amphibian?

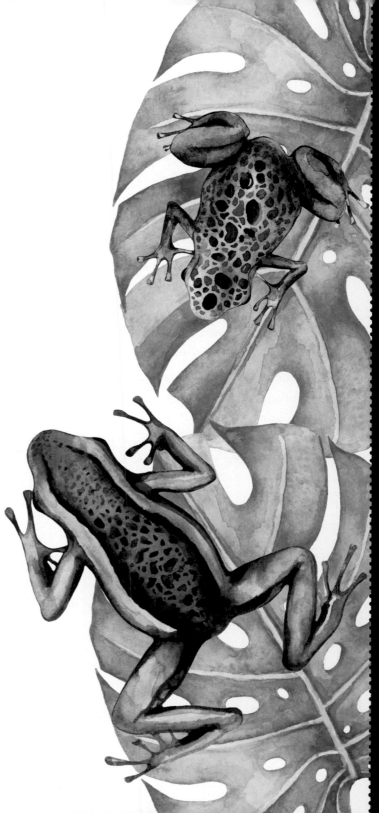

Have you ever heard a bullfrog croak? Or spied a salamander near a stream? Amphibians are all around us, but these shy creatures can be very hard to spot. They need to stay hidden from hungry predators such as birds and snakes. They also need to stay in or near water to keep their skin moist, so it might take a little detective work to track them down.

As you read this book, write down what you've learned in your explorer's notebook (page 3). Then pull out your magnifying glass and follow the clues to find some amphibians near you. Before you get started, though, you should know exactly what an amphibian is—and what it isn't.

Sorting Species

In many ways, scientists are like detectives. They look for clues to solve mysteries. One of these mysteries is how different kinds of animals are related to each other. Which other animals do they most look or act like? And what should we name them? These can be tricky questions. Fortunately, scientists called **taxonomists** are on the case.

Imagine if someone asked you to sort a giant tub of Legos into groups. How would you start? Would you sort them by color? Or maybe by shape or size? Perhaps you could sort them by color first, and then sort those groups by shape and size. Or the

Which of these animals is an amphibian? If you guessed all of them, you're correct! Salamanders, caecilians, and frogs are all types of amphibians.

other way around. This might be trickier than it sounds!

In the same way, taxonomists try to sort all living things into groups that have something in common. They've been at it for more than 2,000 years. A Greek philosopher named Aristotle first came up with a way of grouping animals from simple to more complex. His method was used with only a few changes until the 1700s.

Then scientists began to look for ways to improve it.

In 1758, a Swedish botanist named Carl Linnaeus came up with a better idea. He grouped all living things into large groups, and then divided these groups into smaller and smaller ones based on things they had in common. This basic system of taxonomy is still used today. Even prehistoric fossils can fit into these groups.

AMPHIBIAN SCIENCE

Scientists who study amphibians and reptiles are called herpetologists. This name comes from a Greek word meaning "a creeping thing." Herpetofauna are creepy, crawly animals.

Skeeze/Pixabay

Venu Govindappa/Wikimedia Commons

Bernie/Wikimedia Commons

Make an Explorer's Notebook

Every scientist needs a field notebook to record their observations. Any kind of notebook will work, but it's fun and easy to make your own.

ADULT SUPERVISION REQUIRED

MATERIALS

- 10 sheets of blank or graph paper
- Sheet of cardboard or card stock (8.5 x 11 inches)
- Ruler
- Pencil
- 24 inches (61 cm) embroidery floss
- Large needle

1. Fold the sheet of cardboard or cardstock in half, bringing the shorter edges together.

2. Fold the sheets of paper in half, bringing the shorter edges together. Fit them inside the cover. Trim as needed.

3. With an adult's help, open the book and use a needle to poke three holes along the crease. Place one hole in the center and one about 2.5 inches (6.5 cm) from the center on each side. Wiggle the needle around in each hole to make it larger.

4. Thread a needle with floss (do not separate the strands). Pull about 3 inches (7.6 cm) through the eye of the needle.

5. Push the needle through the center hole to the outside of the book, leaving about 6 inches (15 cm) of string hanging inside.

6. Hold onto the "tail" of string and push the needle in through the top hole.

7. Push the needle out through the lower hole.

8. Thread the needle in through the center hole again.

9. Take the leftover string and the beginning piece and tie them firmly in a knot. Trim off extra string.

10. Decorate your cover however you'd like. You may want to add a piece of colorful washi or duct tape along the edge of the book to reinforce it.

EXPLORER'S NOTEBOOK

Then Linnaeus had another good idea. He started using the names of the two smallest groups that a plant or animal belonged to, the genus and species, as its scientific name. For example, the scientific name for humans is *Homo sapiens*, which comes from Latin words meaning "wise man." These names were in Latin because all scientists at that time used Latin to talk to each other. This way of naming living things is called **binomial nomenclature**. People around the world might call a plant or animal by different common names, which can get confusing, but it only has one scientific name.

Millions of species have been named, and more are being discovered every day. Taxonomists study these new organisms to see where they fit. Today, they can use high-tech tools such as DNA testing to look for clues.

FUN FACT

Some scientific names have a letter L. at the end. That means that they were named by Linnaeus himself.

Growing a Backbone

Using Linnaeus's system, all living things can be sorted into different groups called **kingdoms**. Scientists disagree about how many kingdoms there are, but most say five or six. Amphibians belong to the animal kingdom. So do all other animals with more than one cell.

The animal kingdom can be divided into many smaller groups. Each of these is called a **phylum**. Amphibians belong to phylum Chordata. Animals in this group are called **vertebrates**. Birds, reptiles, fishes, and mammals are also vertebrates. If you run your fingers down the middle of your back, you can feel the bones in your spine. That's because you are a vertebrate too.

All vertebrates have a spinal column at some stage of their life. It is usually made of bone, but in sharks it is made of **cartilage**. You can find out what cartilage feels like by squishing the end of your nose or bending your ear. Cartilage makes these parts of your body soft and flexible. Now tap your head gently. The hard skull you feel is bone.

Animals without backbones are called **invertebrates**. Insects, crabs, snails, and sponges are a few examples. Some, like jellyfish, have soft, squishy bodies. Others,

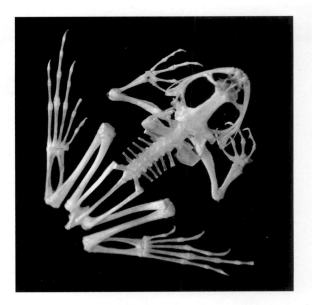

Amphibians, like all vertebrates, have a backbone. This skeleton shows the bones that make up a frog's body. *Amada44/Wikimedia Commons*

like lobsters, have a hard outer shell with a soft body inside.

Can you imagine what you would look like without your bones? How would you move around? A vertebrate's skeleton helps it walk, run, or fly. It gives strength, support, and shape to the body. Bones are lighter and less bulky than the hard outer shells (called exoskeletons) of insects or crabs. Bones do not need to be shed, as a shell does. This is why vertebrates can grow larger than invertebrates, in general.

Besides a backbone, vertebrates have a few other things in common. Their bodies can be divided evenly in half, with each side a mirror image of the other. They never have more than two pairs of legs. If you see a creature with 6, 8, or 10 legs scurry by, it definitely isn't a vertebrate! All vertebrates also have a tail at some stage of their life. Some, like humans, have tails only at an early stage of development, before they are born, or hidden inside their bodies.

What Are Amphibians?

So now you know that amphibians are animals with backbones. But how can you tell a salamander from a lizard, a tadpole from a fish, or a caecilian from a snake?

Amphibians have several things in common that set them apart from other vertebrates. They make up their own class of vertebrates, called Amphibia.

There are three main ways you can identify an amphibian. First, they are cold-blooded—that is, they cannot warm or cool themselves but instead rely on their environment to warm or cool them. Second, amphibians have slimy skin and do not have fur, feathers, or scales. Their thin skin is **permeable**—it lets air and water go through easily. Third, most amphibians spend part of their life in water and part on land. They can do this because

they hatch out in one form and later change to another. This change is called **metamorphosis**.

Now let's take a closer look at some of these amphibian features.

These red-eyed tree frog eggs contain developing embryos. They are attached to the underside of a leaf overhanging a body of water. The tadpoles hatch out and drop into the water, where they will live until they become adults.
Geoff Gallice/Wikimedia Commons

FUN FACT: THE SIX KINGDOMS

All living things can be divided into six large groups called kingdoms. Amphibians belong to kingdom Animalia.

Bacteria*: Bacteria and cyanobacteria
Archaea*: Single-celled organisms that differ from ordinary bacteria; many live in harsh environments
Protista: Most types of algae, slime molds, and single-celled animals called protozoa
Fungi: Mushrooms, yeasts, and other types of fungus
Plantae: Plants with more than one cell
Animalia: Animals with more than one cell

*Some textbooks combine the Bacteria and Archaea into one kingdom, called **Monera**.

In Cold Blood

All amphibians are cold-blooded. That means they cannot make their own heat or cool down their bodies—their temperature matches the air around them. Scientists call this **ectothermy**, because these animals' heat comes from outside their bodies (*ecto-* means outside, and *therm-* means heat).

Warm-blooded animals, such as mammals and birds, are **endothermic** (*endo-* means inside). They make their own heat by burning energy from food. Hair, feathers, or fur help keep them warm, along with a layer of fat under their skin.

Have you ever seen a dog panting on a hot day or felt goose bumps on your arms on a chilly morning? Warm-blooded animals use tricks like shivering and goose bumps to warm up. When their bodies get too warm, they cool down by sweating, panting, or increasing blood flow to the skin so that the blood is cooled.

Cold-blooded creatures can't do any of these things. The main way they change their body temperature is by moving to a warmer or cooler place. In order to be active and digest their food, they need to stay warm—but not so warm they roast! So on a hot day, you may find amphibians lurking in the water, hidden under a shady rock, or burrowed into cool, moist soil. On a cool morning, you might find them basking on a sunny log or lily pad for a short time to warm up.

Some Like It Hot

Some amphibians prefer to stay cool, while others like it hot. The Mount Lyell salamander lives in the mountains of California. It is active even when temperatures are below freezing, at 28°F (–2°C), and seems to prefer relatively cool temperatures (55–57°F [13–14°C]). The waxy monkey frog, on the other hand, doesn't mind temperatures of up to 106°F (41°C). It lives in the steamy tropical forests of South America. The frog

uses its hind legs to spread a waxy secretion over its body. This slows the evaporation of water from its skin and allows the frog to tolerate high temperatures without getting dehydrated. Each of these amphibians is well adapted to its habitat.

Escaping the Extremes

Most amphibians that live in **temperate** climates burrow into the mud of a pond or riverbank in winter. Here they **hibernate** until spring, using the earth's warmth to keep from freezing. The American bullfrog, for example, can hibernate underwater even when the surface water freezes. Its metabolism slows down because of the

The wood frog can survive further north than any other North American frog. It can pump glucose into its cells to keep them from freezing. *Judy Gallagher/ Wikimedia Commons*

cold water temperature, so it can absorb enough oxygen through its skin to meet its needs.

Amphibians in hotter climates, on the other hand, often escape summer heat by hiding under leaves, rocks, or logs. They may also burrow into the ground or hide in rock crevices. This type of "summer hibernation" is called **estivation**.

The North American wood frog has an unusual way of surviving winter. It turns into a frogsicle! Ice forms around its organs and under its skin, and its eyes turn white as its lenses freeze. The frog does not move or breathe, and its heart stops beating.

However, the frog's cells do not actually freeze. They are pumped full of glucose, a type of sugar. The glucose keeps the water in the cells from freezing. This **adaptation** allows the wood frog to live much farther north than other amphibians. It can even be found in the Arctic. In spring, the frog thaws from the inside out. Its heart starts beating, its brain starts working, and then it begins to move its legs. Soon it hops away, as good as new.

Smooth, Slimy Skin

Amphibians do not have fur, feathers, or scales. Their skin is smooth and slimy. It is also very thin. This lets gases such as oxygen pass through. Amphibians can breathe directly through their skin. Most also have lungs or **gills**, but the lungless salamanders, which make up more than two-thirds of all salamander species, breathe entirely through their skin.

Most amphibians can also "drink" through their skin. Many frogs have a special drinking patch on their underside that soaks up water. Toads and salamanders that live in deserts burrow underground and soak up moisture from the soil around them.

Have you ever noticed how your bathroom mirror fogs up after you take a hot shower or bath? The warm water vapor condenses when it hits the cooler surface of the mirror, forming tiny water droplets. The green tree frog of Australia uses this trick to survive in its dry desert habitat. It soaks in the water that condenses on its skin when it hops from the cool night air into a warm burrow.

Pack an Amphibian-Watching Kit

So you want to go amphibian-watching. What should you pack?

MATERIALS

- Waterproof boots
- Binoculars
- Magnifying glass or hand lens
- Field guide to amphibians in your area
- Pond viewer (see page 22)
- Explorer's notebook
- Pencil
- Nitrile gloves (if you plan to handle any amphibians)
- Waterproof bag

Wear your boots, and pack the other items in the waterproof bag. Bring your kit along on your next trip into the field!

Because of their thin, moist skin, amphibians tend to avoid the sun. Most species that live on land come out only at night to hunt and breed, especially on damp, rainy evenings. The darkness not only keeps them cool but also hides them from predators. When animals are only active at night, we call them **nocturnal**.

Slippery Slime

Do you ever put lotion on your hands when your skin feels dry? Amphibians make their own "lotion" to keep their skin moist. Special glands in their skin create a slimy substance called mucus. It is similar to the mucus that plugs up your nose when you have a cold. This mucus keeps the amphibian's skin from drying out. Studies show it may contain chemicals that kill bacteria or fungi as well. This keeps the animal from getting infections. Some frogs create a cocoon of mucus and dead skin before they estivate.

Mucus can serve yet another purpose: to protect an amphibian from predators. When they are stressed, some amphibians make themselves extra slippery and slimy. This makes it harder for the predator to grab them. Mucus is useful stuff!

A Double Life

Amphibians spend part of their lives in water and part on land. Their name comes from the Greek words *amphi*, which means "both," and *bios*, which means "life." They live a double life!

The reason this double life is possible is that most amphibians undergo drastic changes in form as they develop. They lay eggs in or near a body of water. The babies that hatch out are called larvae or tadpoles. They live in the water and breathe through gills, just like fish do. They look a lot like fish too—at least until they start to sprout legs. Many amphibians lose their gills when they become adults. They breathe through their lungs and/or skin. Adult amphibians usually live on land.

Of course, not all amphibians follow these rules. The Mexican axolotl, for example, keeps its feather-like gills and lives underwater all its life. Some salamanders spend their whole lives on land. And a few kinds of frogs can even be found in the desert. However, even these desert-dwellers need moist places to live and lay eggs.

Although they have many things in common, amphibians are a wildly varied bunch. In the next chapter, you'll look at some of the many families of amphibians.

(*left*) A tadpole develops legs and loses its tail as it undergoes metamorphosis. *mvbhaktha/ Wikimedia Commons*

(*right*) The Mexican axolotl salamander never fully develops into a typical adult amphibian form. It keeps its feathery gills and lives underwater all its life. *schlyx/Shutterstock.com*

Change the Freezing Point of Water

Wood frogs can survive in the far north because their cells fill with glucose, a type of sugar. Glucose lowers the freezing point of water. So while the water around them freezes, the frog's cells do not. Water expands when it freezes, so without the glucose the cells would swell and burst, thus killing the frog.

Other substances can have the same anti-freeze effect. This is why road crews sprinkle salt on roads in winter to keep ice from forming, and why people put antifreeze in their cars' engines to keep them from freezing or overheating.

Try this experiment to see for yourself how antifreeze works.

MATERIALS

- Explorer's notebook
- Pen
- 5 clear disposable plastic cups
- Permanent marker
- Tap water
- Sugar
- Salt
- Tablespoon

1. In your explorer's notebook, draw a chart like the one shown here.

2. Label five plastic cups as follows: TAP WATER, 2 T. SUGAR, 4 T. SUGAR, 1 T. SALT, and 2 T. SALT.

3. Measure ½ cup cold tap water into each cup.

4. Set the cup labeled TAP WATER aside. Add sugar and salt to cups in the amounts marked (T. means tablespoon).

5. Stir each mixture well and set all five cups in the freezer.

6. Note the starting time in the time column and describe the contents of each cup in the appropriate column.

7. Check your cups every 15 minutes. Note the state of the water in each cup in your chart. Is it liquid? Slushy? Frozen around the edges? Solid?

8. Once all the cups have frozen, look at your chart. How did adding sugar or salt affect the freezing process? Which cups were the first to freeze? Which were the last?

CHANGE THE FREEZING POINT OF WATER

Title: _____   Date: _____

Time							
Tap water							
2 T. sugar							
4 T. sugar							
1 T. salt							
2 T. salt							

2

Meet the Families

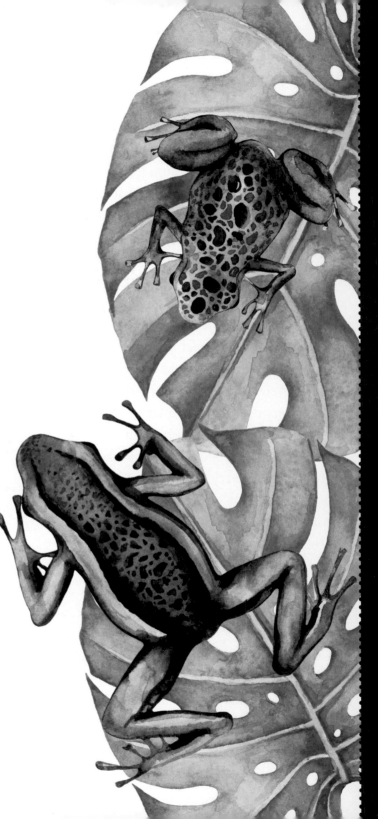

When you hear the word *amphibian*, you most likely picture a frog or toad. Those are the best-known members of class Amphibia. But there are actually three different groups of amphibians—including one that might surprise you.

The first group is order Anura, which includes the frogs and toads. The second is order Caudata, the newts and salamanders. And the last is order Gymnophiona, which is made up of wormlike creatures known as caecilians. Altogether, there are more than 8,000 different kinds of amphibians—far too many to fit in this book!

Order Anura: The Frogs and Toads

Can you imagine having more than 7,000 cousins? Frogs do! Order Anura includes more than 7,000 different species of frogs. Frogs with shorter legs, little to no webbing between their toes, and dry, bumpy skin are commonly known as toads. Those with long hind legs, smooth skin, and webbed toes or large toe pads are called frogs. Technically, though, there is no difference between the two. Scientists usually refer to both frogs and toads as **anurans** to avoid confusion.

New species of anurans are being discovered every day. Nearly a quarter of the species we know about have been discovered since the year 2000. Frogs and toads can be found on every continent except Antarctica.

Most anurans are good jumpers. Some can climb trees with their sticky toe pads, and a few can even glide through the air. Other species prefer to walk or run rather than hop.

The name Anura means "without tails," and adult frogs and toads do not have tails. Two species of frogs—fittingly called tailed frogs—appear to have short tails, but these are actually reproductive organs.

Sticky toe pads help these tree frogs cling to a narrow branch.
Kurit afshen/Shutterstock.com

Like all amphibians, frogs and toads undergo metamorphosis as they develop. Some start off as eggs, hatch out as tadpoles, and then gradually develop legs and lose their tails as they become adults. These frogs and toads live in water for at least part of their life cycle. When they are tadpoles, they have gills that help them breathe underwater. As they grow into adults, the gills are absorbed into their bodies and they grow lungs. Other anurans hatch out as smaller versions of their parents, called froglets.

Frog Families

Now it's time to meet some of the frog families. There are around 30 different families of anurans. Members of these families tend to have some things in common, just like your family members do. That is why taxonomists group them together.

Close your eyes for a moment and picture a frog. What do you see? You probably pictured a small green animal. But frogs actually come in many different sizes and a rainbow of colors, from the bright red strawberry poison dart frog to the blue poison dart frog. Each is perfectly adapted to its habitat.

Tree Frogs

The tree frogs, or Hylidae, make up the largest family of frogs, with nearly 1,000 species identified so far. As you might suspect, these lean, long-legged frogs like to live in trees. Sticky pads on their wide toes help them cling to the bark. They also have extra cartilage in their toes that makes them more flexible than usual. These frogs can walk straight up a tree trunk—or even a glass window. The spring peepers heard in many places in North America belong to the tree frog family.

True Frogs

Another large family of frogs, the Ranidae, is made up of around 400 species. That's a lot of relatives! The Ranidae are known as the "true frogs." Most are either green or shades of brown. They have teeth in the top of their mouths and some webbing in their

---

AMPHIBIAN SCIENCE

A group of frogs is called a *chorus* or an *army*. A group of toads is called a *knot*. And a group of salamanders is called a *herd* or *congress*!

(*left*) Poison dart frogs are among the world's most colorful amphibians. This blue poison dart frog contains enough poison to kill a hundred people. *suju/Pixabay*

(*right*) Male spring peepers puff out their vocal sacs to make a high piping whistle. In spring, a chorus of these tiny frogs can create quite a din! *Brian Lasenby/iStock*

hind toes. Most true frogs are a few inches long, but they can be as small as your pinky fingernail or as big as a house cat. Bullfrogs and leopard frogs belong to this family.

Fleshbelly Frogs

The fleshbelly frogs, or Craugastoridae, are another large family of around 120 species. These frogs live in the southern United States and in Central and South America. Most are shades of brown, which helps them hide in leaf litter or along the edges of streams. Fleshbelly frogs do not have a tadpole stage; they hatch out as small froglets. Their toes do not have any webbing.

The recently discovered *Paedophryne amanuensis* is one of the world's smallest frogs. *Rittmeyer EN, Allison A, Gründler MC, Thompson DK, Austin CC/Wikimedia Commons*

GOLIATH FROG

The world's largest frog belongs to the true frog family. The Goliath frog grows up to 16 inches (41 cm) long and 6.5 pounds (2.9 kg) in weight. It can jump 10 feet (3 m) in a single leap!

Goliath frogs live in the rain forests of Africa, near the equator. They eat insects, crustaceans, fish, and even other amphibians. Because they are hunted for food, Goliath frogs have become endangered.

The Goliath frog is the world's largest frog.
Daniel Heuclin/Minden Pictures

Narrow-Mouthed Frogs

There are more than 600 species in family Microhylidae, the narrow-mouthed frogs. Just as their name suggests, members of this family have pointy heads and narrow mouths. Most have no teeth. These frogs tend to be short and stocky. They can be found on every continent except Europe and Antarctica. Since their mouths are too narrow to eat larger prey, these frogs eat only insects and other tiny animals.

They often use flat spades on their back feet to burrow into the soil when they feel threatened.

One of the world's smallest frogs belongs to this family. It is just 0.27 inches (7 mm) long—about the size of a housefly. *Paedophryne amauensis* lives in Papua New Guinea. It hides in the leaf litter of tropical forests and eats tiny insects.

True Toads

The more than 600 members of the family Bufonidae are called the "true toads." They are warty and toothless. They have short, thick legs and can't jump as far as most frogs—they're better at walking than hopping. Most true toads have glands on their head that make a milky poison. A dog that bites a toad may start to foam at the mouth. In some cases, a toad's poison can kill pets and predators that try to feed on it. A few humans have died from eating poisonous toads or their eggs as well.

True toads are **native** to all warm continents except Australia. The bumps on their skin contain **keratin**, which is the material found in your hair and fingernails. It keeps water from passing through the skin as easily as it does in other frogs. As a result, toads can live in drier climates than frogs can.

Order Caudata: Newts and Salamanders

The next order of amphibians is the salamanders and newts. Salamanders have short legs and long tails. They look a lot like lizards, but instead of being scaly like lizards, their skin is smooth and moist. Their name comes from the Greek word for "fire lizard." Long ago, salamanders were associated with fire because they would crawl out of the logs people tossed on the fire, so many people thought that's where they came from. In reality, the animals were just trying to escape the heat.

Most salamanders are just a few inches long, but a few species can reach nearly 6 feet (1.8 m) in length. There are more than 700 species worldwide, and they live on every continent except Australia and Antarctica. Some live in the water, some live on land, and some live in both places.

Salamanders are **carnivores**. That means they eat meat—specifically, insects,

GLASS FROGS

The glass frog family got its name from the transparent skin on the underside of some of its family members. These frogs' bellies are so clear that their internal organs can be clearly seen through the skin. Some glass frogs have green bones, while others have white ones.

Guayasamin JM, Cisneros-Heredia DF, Maynard RJ, Lynch RL, Culebras J, Hamilton PS/Wikimedia Commons

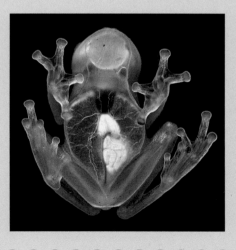

ANCIENT AMPHIBIANS

Dinosaurs get most of the attention, but ancient amphibians were pretty impressive too. The earliest amphibian fossils date to around 190 million years ago. While some resembled today's amphibians, others were much larger. The Beelzebufo (Devil Frog) weighed 10 pounds (4.5 kg) and measured 1.5 feet (46 cm) long. With its wide mouth, it probably munched on the occasional baby dinosaur as well as the giant insects that also lived in its era. The Archegosaurus, on the other hand, looked almost like an alligator. It grew to 10 feet (3 m) in length and weighed several hundred pounds.

This is an artist's concept of what the prehistoric Beelzebufo, or Devil Frog, might have looked like. It is seen here eating a small dinosaur. *Nobu Tamura/Wikimedia Commons*

This drawing shows an artist's concept of what the prehistoric Archegosaurus might have looked like. *Богданов ДиБгд/Wikimedia Commons*

worms, and other small animals. They have teeth on their top and bottom jaws, so they can chew their prey and don't have to swallow it whole, as frogs do.

One surprising thing about salamanders is that many can shed their tails and grow new ones. Some can even grow new legs, hearts, and other organs. Scientists are studying them to figure out how they do this.

Salamander Families

Sirens

If you ever see a siren in the wild, you might think it's an eel—it's an easy mistake to make. These long, thin salamanders in the family Sirenidae have no hind legs (they're the exception to the rule) and very tiny front legs.

Sirens' mud-colored skin matches their favorite habitat—the mud and muck at the bottom of streams and marshes. Their gills let them breathe underwater. Sirens hunt at

Members of the siren family have no hind legs. They spend most of their time underwater. *Farinosa/iStock*

night for aquatic insects, worms, crayfish, and other crustaceans. Once in a while they venture out on land, and they can make soft squeaking noises when they are out of the water.

In dry weather, sirens bury themselves in sand or mud to estivate until the rains return. Some ooze mucus from their skin, which hardens into a cocoon that covers all but their nose. This prevents them from drying out. In this way, they can survive for weeks waiting for wet weather.

Mudpuppies

Like their sirenian relatives, mudpuppies live underwater. These members of the family Proteidae have big red bushy gills, which they keep even as adults. Mudpuppies get their name from the squeaky

Mudpuppies are easy to identify by their big red gills. *Todd Pierson*

Make Your Own Fossil

Fossils are formed over millions of years from vast amounts of pressure. But you can make your own fossil craft in a much shorter time.

MATERIALS

- Small paper bowl
- Modeling clay
- Plaster of Paris
- Water
- Small objects such as seashells, toy animals, etc.

1. Spread modeling clay on the bottom of a bowl.

2. Press small objects into the clay to make prints. Remove the objects.

3. Follow the directions on the box of plaster of Paris to mix up enough to fill the bowl.

4. Pour the prepared plaster into the bowl. Let dry (about an hour).

5. Once the plaster is completely dry, tear away the paper bowl. Carefully remove the clay.

6. Check out your fossils!

How to Identify an Amphibian

Looking for amphibians is fun! But how can you tell if you've found one? It's helpful to bring along an amphibian field guide—a book that lists different kinds of amphibians and ways to identify them. But here are some things to look for to make sure you've got an amphibian in the first place.

🐸 Adult frogs and toads have four legs and smooth or warty skin. They do not have tails. Their eyes bulge out the top of their head.

🐸 Tadpoles (juvenile amphibians) look almost like fish. They have large heads and flattened tails. But their fins are different from those of a fish. Tadpoles only have fins on their tails, not on their bodies as fish do. As they grow, tadpoles gradually grow legs and lose their tails.

🐸 Salamanders look almost like lizards. But their skin is smooth rather than scaly. Their toes are webbed, while most reptiles have claws. To tell salamanders apart, scientists look for markings on their skin, the shape of their heads and bodies, the number of costal grooves (folds on the sides of their bodies), and details about their teeth and mouths.

🐸 Caecilians look similar to earthworms or small snakes. Their bodies have rings, like earthworms'. But unlike worms, caecilians have jaws and teeth as well as a backbone. Their skin is smooth, not scaly like a snake's skin.

Frog

smooth skin (frog)
warty skin (toad)

four legs

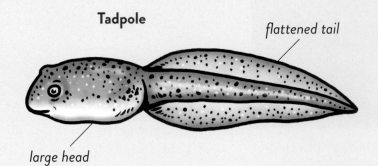

Tadpole

flattened tail

large head

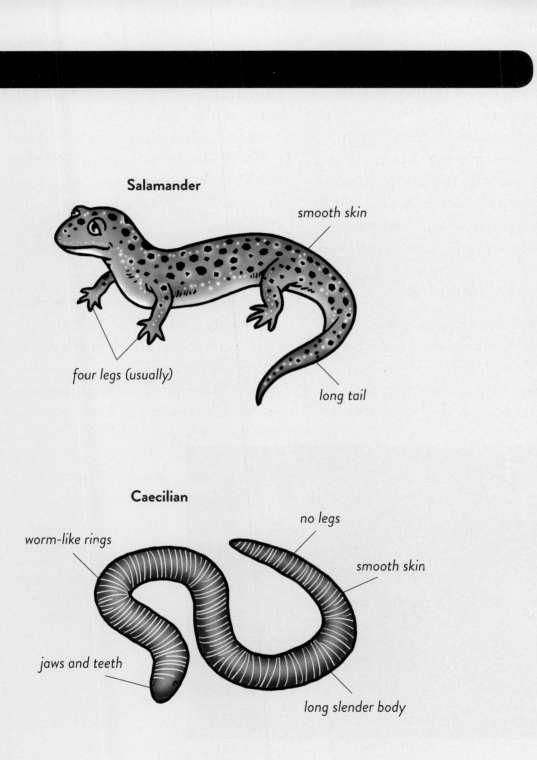

Salamander

smooth skin

four legs (usually)

long tail

Caecilian

no legs

worm-like rings

smooth skin

jaws and teeth

long slender body

sounds they make, which sound a bit like a puppy barking. Some people call them "waterdogs" for the same reason.

Mudpuppies hide under rocks, logs, and vegetation and come out at night to hunt for crayfish, worms, and snails. They can grow to more than 16 inches (41 cm) in length. Mudpuppies live in the eastern half of the United States and Canada.

Olms

Olms are so strange looking that long ago, people thought olms were baby dragons! Their skin has no pigment, so it appears pinkish because of the blood vessels beneath it. These salamanders live in underground caves in Slovenia and Croatia. They have tiny legs and can grow up to a foot long. And because they live in the dark, olms are blind. Scientists believe olms can live for 100 years or more.

Amphiumas

Amphiumas look almost like snakes. But if you look closely, you will see four tiny legs. These long, thin salamanders are sometimes called "congo eels," even though they aren't eels at all. They can grow up to 36 inches (91 cm) long.

Amphiumas live in swampy areas and feed on crayfish, small fish, insects, and other small animals. Sometimes they even eat each other! When an amphiuma attacks its prey, it takes a big bite and rolls around, thrashing around like a crocodile in a death roll. Few predators except snakes will eat amphiumas, perhaps because of the slimy mucus that oozes out of their skin when they are threatened.

Newts

Scientists have identified about 80 different species of newts, which are in the family Pleurodelinae. Newts are a group of salamanders with rough skin. Young newts are called efts. They live on land. Some adult newts live in water, while others live on land. These species return to the water each year to breed.

Newts can produce poison either in their skin or in poison glands. The most toxic ones tend to be brightly colored. The colors warn predators that they are not good to eat.

Mole Salamanders

Mole salamanders live in North America, from Canada to Mexico. These chubby salamanders burrow into the ground or leaf litter like moles, hence their name. They come out only to breed in the spring, often in large numbers.

Mole salamanders are often brightly colored and can grow to 13.8 inches (35 cm) in length. One of the best-known members of this group is the Mexican axolotl, which never develops into an adult form but keeps its gills and stays in the water all its life.

Lungless Salamanders

Just as their name suggests, lungless salamanders have no lungs. So how do they breathe? Through their skin! Gases can pass through these animals' thin, moist skin and the lining of their mouths. They must stay damp at all times so they can breathe. That's why they only come out in damp weather, usually at night.

Most lungless salamanders live in temperate climates in the northern hemisphere. Some burrow into the ground near streams or lakes, others live in caves, and still others climb trees.

Giant Salamanders

There are only three members of the giant salamander family, but they are truly giant. Giant salamanders feed on fish, worms, insects, crayfish, snails, and even smaller salamanders. The largest species live in China and Japan. Chinese giant

The spring salamander lives in cold springs in the eastern United States. It belongs to the lungless salamander family. *Jay Ondreicka/Shutterstock.com*

CHINESE GIANT SALAMANDER

At first glance, you might mistake this large aquatic creature for an alligator. But it's actually a salamander—a very, very big one! The Chinese giant salamander lives in the hill streams of central and southern China. It can grow to 6 feet (1.8 meters) in length. In other words, this salamander might be longer than you are!

In 2015, a Chinese fisherman found a giant salamander that weighed 114 pounds (53 kilograms) living in a cave. These giants live an average of 80 years in the wild. Unfortunately, the number of Chinese giant salamanders has dropped by 80 percent since 1960. They have suffered from loss of habitat and pollution as well as people hunting them for food and to breed on farms.

tristan tan/iStock

salamanders can reach 6 feet (1.8 m) in length! Hellbenders, also called "devil dogs," are not far behind. These large salamanders live in streams in the eastern and central United States. They range from 12 to 29 inches long (30 to 74 cm). Their wrinkled, brownish-gray skin has black spots. They hide under stones during the day and creep out at night to feed.

Caecilians

The last and most mysterious group of amphibians is order Gymnophiona, the caecilians. If you've never seen a caecilian, you're not alone—few people in the world have ever encountered one. These shy creatures live underground in swampy tropical regions of South America, Asia, and Africa.

Long and legless, caecilians look like giant earthworms and are so flexible they can tie themselves into knots. Some people call them "rubber eels."

There are around 200 known species of caecilians. They range from 3.5 inches (9 cm) to nearly 5 feet (1.5 m) in length. Many are brown, but they can also be blue, purple, green, orange, or yellow. Some have stripes or blotches. The bright colors of these creatures may be **aposematic**, which means that they serve as a warning sign to

3

Parts of an Amphibian

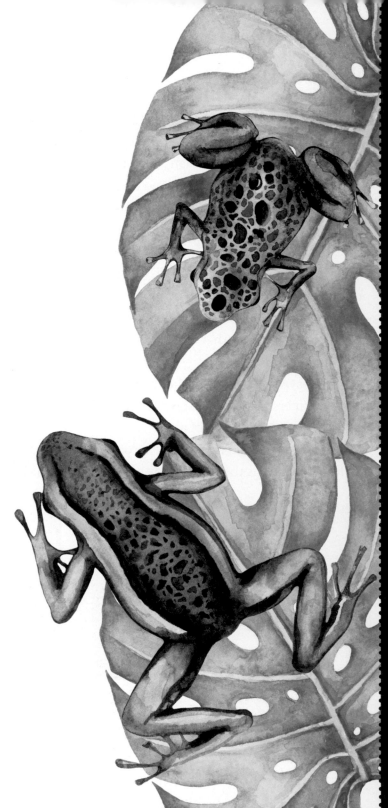

Have you ever noticed how your fingers and toes get wrinkly after a long bath or swim? If you stay in the water too long, you start to look as wrinkled as a raisin! Humans are adapted to living on land, not in the water. Amphibians, on the other hand, are adapted to living both on land and in the water. In this chapter, we will look at some of these adaptations.

Peter Trimming/Wikimedia Commons

The Eyes Have It

Can you open your eyes underwater? It takes some practice, and it can be painful if the water isn't clean. Amphibians need to be able to see well both underwater and on land at different points in their life cycle, so their eyes are specially adapted for that lifestyle.

Like fish, amphibians have a clear membrane covering their eyes that adds extra protection. Amphibians that live in the water, including larval forms like tadpoles, have no eyelids. Those that live on land have short eyelids.

Frogs have excellent eyesight—these hungry hunters need to spot prey. Their bulging eyes can see straight ahead, to the sides, and even behind their heads. Frogs can focus on things that are nearby as well as things that are far away. Special glands keep their eyeballs moist at all times.

Salamanders also have bulgy eyes, but they are smaller than a frog's and located farther down on the animal's head. Salamanders do not see as much detail as we do, but they can see in color and can even see ultraviolet light, which is a wavelength that humans cannot see.

Salamanders' eyes are well adapted for night vision, since that is when salamanders usually hunt. Species that live in water are farsighted when they are in the water and nearsighted on land.

If you lived in the dark, your eyes wouldn't be very useful. Amphibians that live in dark environments don't need to see much either. Caecilians, for instance, spend their lives underground where eyes are mostly useless. The word caecilian means "blind," and although caecilians do have eyes, they're very small and hidden beneath layers of skin. The skin helps to protect their eyes from the rough soil. Caecilian eyes can sense light but not much else. Many caecilians can sense light with their skin too. Instead of eyes, these animals rely on two small feelers between their eyes and nose to find their prey.

Super Slimy Skin

Have you ever gotten chapped lips or hands? This can happen when you have to wash your hands a lot or when the air is extremely dry. Amphibian skin is very thin and fragile. To keep their skin from getting chapped or scraped up, many amphibians

A frog's eyeballs not only help it see, they also help it swallow by pushing food down its throat. *Nick Harris/Flickr*

The eye of this red-eyed tree frog is covered by a membrane when it is at rest. *Mark Kostich/ iStock*

Caecilian eyes are small and covered with skin. Caecilians cannot see well. *reptiles4all/Shutterstock.com*

Changing Colors

Although they don't change colors as dramatically as chameleons do, some amphibians have skin that turns darker when it is cold. This helps them stay warm, since darker colors can absorb more heat energy from the sun.

Other amphibians change color when it is time to breed. Males of these species change colors for a short time—just a few hours or a few days—during breeding season. Scientists believe males do this to scare off other males.

Some frogs, such as spring peepers, can also change colors to match their background as camouflage.

A Breath of Fresh Air

Most young amphibians and some adults breathe through gills, like fish. Gills generally work in the same way as your lungs do—they absorb oxygen and get rid of carbon dioxide. Inside the gills are thin membranes that allow oxygen from the water to pass through them and into the bloodstream. At the same time, carbon dioxide is removed from the bloodstream and passes out of the gills.

Most amphibians' gills are inside their bodies, so the only part that shows on

coat themselves with slime that comes from special slime glands.

The reason that amphibians need such thin skin is that it allows both oxygen and water to pass through. Toads often live in dry environments where there are no pools of water to drink from, so the ability to soak up water from the soil is particularly useful to them.

Shedding Their Skin

Just like your skin, a frog's skin is constantly replacing itself. The difference is that your skin cells drop off one at a time, so you don't notice any change. A frog, on the other hand, grows a whole new skin under the outer, dead layer. Every week or so, the frog wiggles around to loosen the dead skin, nibbles the skin around its mouth, then pulls the rest over its head like a sweater and eats it. This may sound disgusting to us, but it lets the frog to recycle the salts and nutrients in the skin. Salamanders and caecilians shed their skins as well, and some of them also eat the skin afterward.

Make Your Own Frog Slime

MATERIALS

- 1 cup hot water
- ½–1 teaspoon borax
- 1 bottle white school glue, 5–6 oz.
- ½ cup water
- Green food coloring
- 2 mixing bowls
- Whisk

1. Put 1 cup of hot water and ½ teaspoon of borax in a mixing bowl.

2. Stir until the borax is dissolved.

3. In another bowl, mix 1 bottle of glue with ½ cup water. Beat with a whisk until it is smooth.

4. Add 3 drops of green food coloring to the glue mixture.

5. Pour the glue mixture into the borax mixture. Stir well. Keep stirring or squish with your fingers until the slime absorbs as much of the water as possible.

6. Remove the slime from the bowl and knead it some more. Now it is ready to play with!

the outside is a series of slits behind their heads. However, a few species have big frilly gills on the outside of their heads.

Some amphibians lose their gills and develop lungs when they grow up. Others have both lungs and gills as adults. Members of the lungless salamander family have no gills or lungs as adults. They breathe and take in water through their skin. Some members of this family start off with gills and then lose them. Others skip this larval step altogether. From the time they hatch, they look like mini versions of their parents.

Fancy Feet

What are feet good for? Smelly or not, your feet are very useful. They help support your body and allow you to walk, run, skip, and jump. In the same way, amphibians' feet help them climb, dig, hop, or swim. They are shaped differently depending on the animal's habitat and lifestyle.

Aquatic frogs usually have large, webbed hind feet. When they swim, they kick their feet and then glide forward. Their big feet push them along like a diver's flippers.

Other anurans, like the spadefoot toads, burrow into the ground. They use their hind feet to scrape and scoop the soil. One toe is larger than the others and acts like

The black-webbed tree frog spreads out its toes to parachute from a tree branch to the ground. *Rosa Jay/Shutterstock.com*

a spade. Most of these frogs burrow backward—that way they can watch for predators and prey while they are digging.

Frogs that live on land jump, while toads hop. If there were an amphibian Olympics, the gold medal for the long jump would go to the Australian rocket frog, which can leap up to 50 times its own body length in a single jump. Many frogs can jump 10 to 20 times their own body length. The "true toads," on the other hand, can only hop about three to five times their own body length.

In the Trees

Plop! Plop! Plop! It's raining frogs in the rain forest!

Every morning, Malabar gliding frogs spread their wide, webbed feet and parachute from the tops of the trees to the ground. These frogs have such large feet that they can actually glide through the air. Extra flaps of skin on their legs help catch the air as well. They are one of several species of frogs that can glide.

Many frogs and salamanders are good at climbing trees. Climbing amphibians usually have longer, more slender bodies and legs than their cousins that live on the ground or in water. Special pads on their feet, toes, and tails help them grip the bark.

The toes of some species are sticky, while others form a sort of suction cup. Mucus glands on the feet of tree-climbing species produce mucus that makes them even stickier. Some salamanders even have **prehensile** tails to help them hold on, like a monkey.

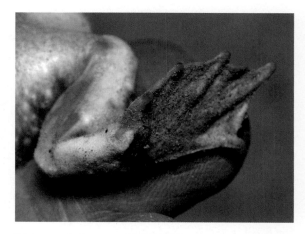

This spadefoot toad's hind feet are handy digging tools thanks to the **keratinized** "spades" on its hind feet. *Gary Nafis*

Lead a Game of Leapfrog

Have you ever played the game of leapfrog? This game has a long history—it's been around since at least the 1500s. The French call it *saute-mouton* (leap-sheep), the Romanians call it *capra* (goat), and the Dutch refer to it as *haasje-over* (hare-over). In India, it is known as *Aar Ghodi Ki Par Ghodi* (horseleap). Each version is slightly different from the others, but the basic idea is the same: to form a moving line by leaping over the backs of the players in front of you.

To start the game, one player crouches low with their head down and feet tucked in. The next player runs up, places their hands on the first player's back, and leaps over them with their legs straddling the player. When they land, they then crouch down. The third player hops over both the first and second players, then crouches down. Players continue to add to the line. When the last one has leaped over everyone, the person at the back stands up and leaps over the line.

A fun variation is to have a leapfrog race. Break your group into two teams of the same size and see which team can leapfrog to the finish line first.

Super Sniffers

Almost all adult amphibians hunt animals for food, so they need sharp senses to help them find their prey. Amphibians also use their senses to find and communicate with others of their species.

Amphibians have a good sense of smell, which is especially useful for animals that hunt in the dark. The Italian cave newt, for instance, uses its finely tuned sense of smell to find its prey and snag it with its tongue in complete darkness.

Along with their nostrils, amphibians also have an organ in the roof of their mouth that helps them smell, called a Jacobson's organ. Snakes and other reptiles have this organ as well. The Jacobson's organ contains lots of nerves and helps the animal sense larger molecules like **pheromones**. Based on the odors it picks up, a salamander can tell the species and sex of other nearby salamanders, as well as whether or not they are prospective mates. Many of these odors come from **feces**.

Can You Hear Me Now?

Frogs mainly use sound to communicate with each other. They have two flat **tympanums**, or eardrums, behind their eyes that help them hear other frogs' calls. These work the same way your eardrums do.

A good way to tell male and female frogs apart is to look at the size of the tympanum. A male frog's tympanum is larger than his eyes, while a female's is the same size as her eyes or smaller.

Male frogs make special calls to attract females during the breeding season. They make different calls to warn other males away from their territory. A third type of call is the distress call, which is given when predators attack. This sharp call might startle the predator into letting go or even attract a still larger predator that might come and eat the attacker.

Toad Talk

Frogs and toads can be quite noisy at certain times of the year. Some people enjoy the sound of this amphibian choir, while others can't stand it. In the 17th century, French nobility sent peasants into the swamps to try to quiet the frogs that were disturbing their sleep. More recently, scientists measured calls of the Puerto Rican coqui frog and found that they are nearly as loud as a jackhammer.

So what is all the racket about? Male frogs and toads croak to attract mates and warn other males to stay away from their territory. Their calls can sound like a banjo, clicking pebbles, a rubber band twanging, or chuckling old men. These different calls help other frogs (and scientists) tell which species is calling.

Frogs also use signals to talk with others in their social group or warn them that a predator is near. These signals can be sounds or movements such as waving or tapping their feet or spreading their toes to flash the colors like a flag. Frogs can communicate with chemicals too. Chemicals

ALL PUFFED UP

In order to make those big sounds, male frogs fill their large vocal sacs with air. They look like large pouches or bubbles. They help make the frog's call louder, just like an inflated balloon amplifies sound. You can test this out by blowing up a balloon and flicking it with your finger.

Some vocal sacs are quite large—even larger than the frog itself. Female frogs do not have vocal sacs, but some can produce soft calls in response to males.

A frog's large flat eardrum is called a tympanum. It is located behind the eye.
Carl D. Howe/Wikimedia Commons

Amphibian Tracks

Many amphibians are shy and nocturnal, so it can be difficult to find them during the daytime. But if you can't find an amphibian, maybe you can find its tracks. Since amphibians often live near water, look along the banks of a pond or stream for signs of amphibian activity. Here are a few clues to look for.

FROGS AND TOADS

Most frogs and toads have four toes on their front feet and five on their hind feet. Frogs tend to jump, while toads tend to walk or take short hops, so looking at the pattern of the tracks can help distinguish between the two. The front feet usually turn inward, and the hind feet turn outward. A toad's toes are usually shorter and thicker than those of a frog.

SALAMANDERS

Like frogs, most salamanders have four toes in front and five in back. All four feet tend to be about the same size. Unlike lizards, they walk slowly. Some drag their tails, leaving long lines in the earth.

bullfrog tracks

toad tracks or tracks made from a smaller frog
(pattern would help determine)

salamander tracks
(front toe marks obscured)

called pheromones signal that a frog is looking for a mate or that it is marking its territory.

The Lateral Line System

Another interesting organ that can be found in aquatic amphibians is the lateral line system. Fish also have this organ. The lateral line system consists of hairlike cells on the head and body that can sense changes in the direction of water currents or changes in pressure. This system allows an African clawed frog, for example, to sense the movement of an insect swimming by so it can quickly catch it.

Turning Tail

What good is a tail? Is it just for show? For amphibians, the answer is a definite no! Amphibians rely on their tails to help them

swim when they are in the water and balance when they are on land.

For certain salamanders, having a tail may even be a lifesaver. If a predator attacks, the salamander can shed its tail. While the predator is distracted with this tasty tidbit, the salamander makes its escape. It later grows a new tail to replace the one it lost.

This salamander is in the process of losing its tail. Salamanders can shed their tails when they feel threatened.
Gary Nafis

4

Amphibians Around the World

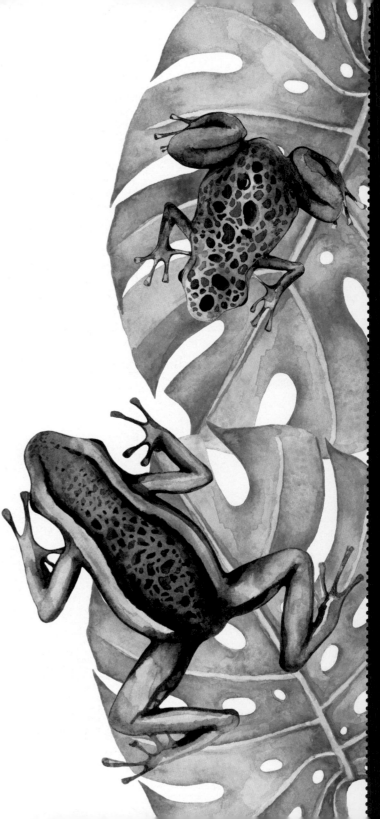

Amphibians can be found on almost every continent in the world. But because of their thin, moist skin, there a few places amphibians simply cannot survive.

One of these places is in salt water. Because an amphibian's skin lets water and air pass through easily, if an amphibian were placed in salt water, water would flow out of its body. Water tends to flow toward areas with a higher concentration of salts, sugars, etc. So, the amphibian would soon become dehydrated and die. For this reason, few, if any, amphibians can be found near oceans and salt marshes.

klimkin/Pixabay

A second place amphibians cannot survive is in deserts that are extremely dry. There is simply not enough water in these habitats to keep the animals and their eggs from drying out.

The last place you won't find any amphibians is near the North and South Poles, which are covered with snow and ice year-round. Not only would they freeze to death, but all the fresh water there is frozen, so the animals cannot drink it. These regions are basically cold deserts since no fresh water is available. Few land animals can survive in these harsh, icy climates.

Where to Find an Amphibian

You might be wondering where you can find an amphibian. The answer is, almost anywhere. But amphibians tend to be shy and nocturnal, so they're not easy to spot.

Look around your area. If you were an amphibian, where would you want to live? Is there a pool of water or a damp rotting log nearby? Scout out the best amphibian habitat and then look for tracks in the mud, or carefully look under a rotting log or large rock. Unless you live in the Arctic or in a desert, there are probably some amphibians living nearby. A park or pond is a good place to look. Damp, cool evenings are the best time to spot amphibians.

Visit the habitat at night in spring or early summer to listen for frog calls. When you hear a call, move around to several spots to help pinpoint its location. Then use a flashlight to look for the animal. An even better way to find the spot is to triangulate it. Have three people spread out and point their flashlights toward the sound. Move to the point where the beams meet and then listen again.

Home Sweet Home

Amphibians live in many different kinds of habitats. Some live in wetlands; others prefer the rain forest. A few even live in the desert. These species either live near water sources or bury themselves deep in the sand for most of the year. However, about 80 percent of frog and toad species

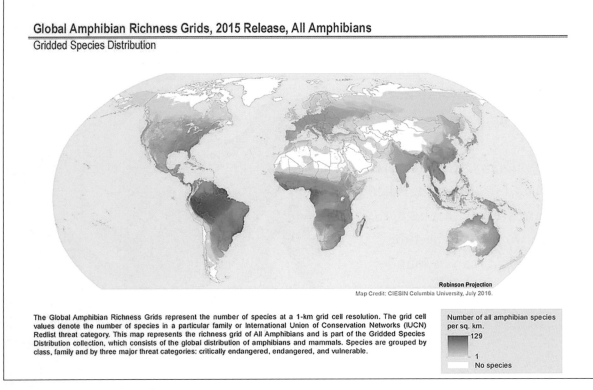

Global Amphibian Richness Grids, 2015 Release, All Amphibians
Gridded Species Distribution

Robinson Projection
Map Credit: CIESIN Columbia University, July 2016.

The Global Amphibian Richness Grids represent the number of species at a 1-km grid cell resolution. The grid cell values denote the number of species in a particular family or International Union of Conservation Networks (IUCN) Redlist threat category. This map represents the richness grid of All Amphibians and is part of the Gridded Species Distribution collection, which consists of the global distribution of amphibians and mammals. Species are grouped by class, family and by three major threat categories: critically endangered, endangered, and vulnerable.

Number of all amphibian species per sq. km.
129
1
No species

Map of worldwide amphibian distribution. *NASA Socioeconomic Data and Applications Center (SEDAC)*

The water-holding frog of Australia makes a mucus cocoon around itself and burrows into the ground during hot weather. It stores water in its bladder. *Tnarg 12345/Wikimedia Commons*

live in the tropics and subtropics, where the climate is warm and damp all year round. These biomes make the perfect home for these thin-skinned, cold-blooded creatures.

Only a small number of amphibians spend their entire lives in water. But many live near bodies of water and lurk around the edges so that they can dive in quickly if they need to escape. Others live under rotting logs or in caves.

Some rain forest frogs spend their whole lives in trees and rarely, if ever, touch the ground. They lay their eggs in pitcher-shaped plants called bromeliads. Water collects in the leaves of these plants, and the tadpoles develop in these tiny pools.

Spadefoot toads, on the other hand, dig burrows in the ground. They can live there for months or even years, waiting for rain.

Wherever they live, amphibians need to stay moist. Species that don't live in or near water have developed some interesting ways to get water. Some absorb it through a thin patch of skin on their belly and thighs by just sitting on damp soil. This pelvic patch has lots of blood vessels in it. These animals can take in as much as 80 percent of the water they need through this patch.

Other species store extra water in their bladder for later use. One of the most amazing examples of this is the water-holding frog. This Australian frog can survive for up to five years underground using only the water stored in its bladder. When water is needed, it moves through the wall of the bladder into the body. Aboriginal people traditionally used the frog as a source of drinking water in the desert, since the water is easy to squeeze out.

Not Too Cold, Not Too Hot

In the story of "Goldilocks and the Three Bears," young Goldilocks finds the bears' porridge too hot, too cold, and finally just right. Finding just the right temperature is important to amphibians too.

Because they are cold-blooded, living in cold places is a big challenge. Some get around this problem by hibernating deep underground in winter, below the frost line. They burrow into the mud, their temperature drops, and their body functions slow down. They enter a deep sleep called **torpor**.

Other amphibians avoid freezing by making a type of antifreeze in their blood. Just like the antifreeze in your car keeps the coolant from freezing, chemicals in a frog's blood can keep the water in its body from freezing at its usual freezing point of 32°F (0°C). That way, its cells do not freeze and burst. The North American wood frog uses this trick to survive even above the Arctic Circle.

Hot, dry weather can be just as dangerous as cold weather for thin-skinned amphibians, so many species estivate. Some of these species make a special mucus membrane that hardens into a cocoon. This crusty coating keeps the animal from drying out and allows it to survive for months or even years under hot, dry conditions.

Amphibians on the Move

Many amphibians move from place to place at certain times of the year. Some migrate short distances between their summer and winter habitats, and many travel to breeding ponds in spring. Amphibians tend to return to the same pond or stream where they were born when it is time to lay their eggs. However, a few individuals may travel to other ponds instead. That way they can increase gene flow between populations, which helps the species to survive and adapt. Some species travel up to 9 miles (14 km) when they migrate.

In cooler climates, hundreds or even thousands of salamanders migrate to breeding ponds at the same time on damp spring nights. This can be a dangerous journey. When they have to cross roads along the way, large numbers of animals can be killed at once. In some areas, police close off roads and volunteers help direct traffic to protect the salamanders as they travel.

Invasion of the Toads!

While amphibians don't usually travel long distances on their own, humans often move them around the world, either accidentally

Salamander Crossing

If you live in a place where salamanders migrate in the spring, don't miss the chance to watch them travel to their breeding ponds! Check with your local nature center or park service to find out when and where the migration is expected to happen. Many parks will add you to a mailing list and notify you when migration starts.

Since it will likely be a chilly, damp night when the salamanders migrate, you'll want to dress warmly and wear rubber boots. You'll need an umbrella and flashlight as well. Just be sure not to disturb the salamanders on this very important journey. If you go hiking a lot, it is also a good idea to clean your boots after each visit to make sure you aren't transporting diseases from one place to another.

or on purpose. Animals are introduced to new areas as food sources, to eat pests, or as pets. Eggs can be carried accidentally on boat hulls, in ship ballast water, on plants, or in soil.

Most animals that arrive in a new habitat do not survive, but if conditions are just right, they may make themselves right at home. Then they may become a problem. We call these animals **invasive species**. Invasive species can take food and other resources away from native species and may carry diseases. Because they often have no natural predators in their new habitats, they can spread quickly and even threaten whole ecosystems.

Several kinds of amphibians have become invasive in certain parts of the world. One of these is the cane toad. This toad, which is native to Central and South America, was brought to Australia to help control a pesky beetle that was damaging sugarcane crops. But not only did the toads fail to eat the beetles, they quickly became pests themselves. Today, there are millions of cane toads in Australia. Pets as well as native snakes, lizards, and other predators are often sickened or killed when they try to eat these highly toxic animals.

The state of Florida seems to be a hot spot for invasive species, including amphibians. The problem began when the greenhouse frog arrived from the West Indies in 1863 and quickly replaced native species in the area. Other Florida invaders include the coqui and the large Cuban treefrog, which eats smaller native species of treefrogs. Cane toads have also invaded Florida.

IT'S AN INVASION!

Invasive coqui frogs in Hawaii call so loudly that people living nearby cannot sleep! In some areas, sprays of caffeine, citric acid, and steam are used to kill the frogs. Another troublesome invader is the Cuban treefrog, which has been known to cause power outages. The frogs are attracted to the buzzing noise of transformers and can cause them to short circuit.

The cane toad is an invasive species that can be deadly to native wildlife and pets. *Alex Popovkin/ Wikimedia Commons*

If You Were a Frog

MATERIALS

- Explorer's notebook
- Pen or pencil
- Colored pencils or markers (optional)

Can you imagine what life would be like if you were a frog? Consider the possibilities!

1. If you were a frog, what kind would you be? Would you be big or small? Green, purple, or blue? Spotted or speckled? Would you match your habitat, or flash bright colors to scare predators away? Draw a picture of your froggy self in your explorer's notebook.

2. If you were a frog, where would you live? Would you choose a rain forest or desert? A pond or rotting log? How about a pond to lay your eggs in? Where would you shelter from the heat and the cold? How would you stay safe from predators? Draw a habitat around your frog for it to live in.

3. If you were a frog, what would you eat? Look around the habitat you've drawn. Where would you find food? How would you catch it? Make sure to add some food sources to your habitat as well.

Frogs and Humans

For thousands of years, amphibians have been revered as symbols of transformation, fertility, healing, resurrection, and good luck.

In Ancient Egypt, four gods had frog-like heads. Together with four snake-headed goddesses, the story goes, these gods created the world. One of them, Amun, eventually became the chief god of Egypt. Others continued to play major roles, including Heh, the god of infinity and

TOADSTONES

In the Middle Ages, many people believed that toads produced "toadstones," which could cure many diseases. Early scientists spent many hours searching for these legendary stones. In 1609, royal physician Anselm Boetius de Boodt finally concluded, after spending many long hours observing toads, that this legend was simply nonsense.

time, and Heqet, the goddess of childbirth and fertility. The early Greeks and Romans, Incans, Aztecs, and Mayans also valued frogs as symbols.

Frogs were important in Asian cultures as well. Even today, Japanese travelers sometimes carry frog amulets, or charms, to ensure a safe return. In China, the frog spirit is thought to encourage healing and good fortune. And in some parts of India, frogs are associated with the monsoon rains. Frog marriage ceremonies have even been performed to encourage the rain gods to send rain!

Frogs in Folk Medicine

Take one frog, and call me in the morning. Can you imagine getting a prescription like that from your doctor?

If you had lived long ago, you might have. Frogs have been used in folk medicine for thousands of years. If you had lived in the Middle Ages, you could have attended the annual toad fair in Dorsetshire, England, where various charms and medicines were sold. Amphibian remedies were popular in Asia as well.

Modern science suggests that these ancient remedies actually may have had some value. Studies show that chemicals

found in frog skin may be useful in treating cancer, lessening pain, and treating stomach ulcers. However, not all folk medicines actually have any effect, and taking them can be dangerous. Collecting large numbers of animals from the wild for this use can harm local populations of amphibians too.

Froggy Weather

Perhaps because they were associated with damp, rainy conditions, during medieval times frogs became connected to the weather in people's minds. Some believed that if frogs called especially loudly, storms were sure to follow. It wasn't much of a leap for people to begin using them to try to control the weather. Toads were thrown

into boiling water in an attempt to "brew up" rain through witchcraft.

As with much ancient lore, there was a kernel of truth to this idea that frogs could predict the weather. Tree frogs do call more loudly on warm, still evenings than on cold, windy nights. They may also perch higher up on branches when the sun is shining and the temperature is comfortable. But as for the rest—that was just poppycock!

Once Upon a Frog . . .

Frogs are popular characters in literature and cinema—Kermit the Frog, the naughty Mr. Toad of *The Wind in the Willows*, the best friends in the Frog and Toad books, and Beatrix Potter's *Jeremy Fisher*, to name a few. And where would a fairy tale princess be without a frog prince to kiss?

The Frog Prince is one of the many amphibian characters in literature. *jill111/Pixabay*

Visit a Pond

With an adult, visit a pond in each season, if possible. Sit in the same spot each time. Make careful observations and answer the following questions in your explorer's notebook.

MATERIALS

- Explorer's notebook
- Pen or pencil

1. What kinds of plants and animals do you see?

2. What do you hear?

3. What do you smell?

4. Sketch a picture of the pond.

At the end of the year, you can look back at your notes to see how the pond changed throughout the year.

5

What's on the Menu?

When you picture a carnivore, or "meat eater," you might think of a tiger or lion. But most adult amphibians are carnivores too. They will eat almost anything that moves and will fit in their mouth.

Amphibians can't really chew, so the size of their mouth limits the size of their prey. Narrow-mouthed species feast on small animals such as insects, worms, and slugs. Those with wider mouths may eat fish, small rodents, reptiles, or even other amphibians.

(left) This American bullfrog will eat almost anything it can fit in its wide mouth. *Bruce MacQueen/ Shutterstock.com*

(right) Narrow-mouthed frogs like this one can only eat small animals. *Lja2011/Wikimedia Commons*

Don't Eat Your Brother!

Tadpoles mainly munch on algae, bacteria, and plant material. They filter them out of the water or scrape them off surfaces. Salamander larvae, on the other hand, are mostly carnivores. They hunt tiny zooplankton when they are small, and move on to larger prey as they grow.

Both tadpoles and salamanders sometimes eat other amphibian larvae—even those belonging to their own species. **Cannibalism** often occurs in small ponds when food is limited and larvae are crowded, especially among tiger salamanders and spadefoot toads. Some species avoid eating their own siblings, while others actually prefer them.

On the Hunt

Before an amphibian can eat, it first has to catch its meal. Amphibians that live in water hunt like little vacuum cleaners. They puff out their cheeks and then open their mouths suddenly. This creates a vacuum, and water is sucked in. Any small organisms that might be nearby get sucked in too.

Some amphibians that live on land stalk their food. These animals tend to hunt at night. If they do hunt during the day, they are usually toxic, like the poison dart frogs, and are brightly colored to keep daytime predators away. Some may sneak up slowly on their prey. Others make a flying leap to snag flying insects in midair.

Other amphibians sit and wait for food to wander by. These species tend to hunt during the daytime. They have cryptic coloration, which means that they blend in with their surroundings. They hide in places that their victims are likely to visit. For example, the yellow-striped reed frog lurks in arum lily flowers. It changes color to camouflage itself. When an unsuspecting insect stops by for a sip of nectar, the frog gobbles it up.

Some amphibians take this sit-and-wait strategy a step further. They use sneaky

A Menu for Café Amphibia

Let's say you decide to open a restaurant called Café Amphibia. It will cater to the coolest critters in town: the amphibians. What should you serve these discerning diners? Create a menu for your café. Be creative!

MATERIALS

- Sheet of paper or card stock
- Pen
- Markers or colored pencils

1. Brainstorm items for your menu.

2. List the main categories:
   - Appetizers
   - Main Dishes
   - Soups and Salads
   - Desserts
   - Beverages

3. Add descriptions and prices for each menu item.

4. Draw and color a border around your menu.

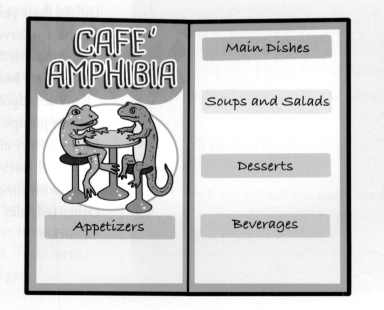

tricks to lure their prey closer. For instance, the cane toad and horned frog attract smaller frogs by twitching their toes. The little frogs think they've spotted something to eat. When they come closer—*zap!*—they become dinner instead.

Do Toads Have Teeth?

Have you ever seen a frog's teeth? They are only found on its upper jaw. Toads do not have teeth. Either way, though, anurans don't do much chewing.

To catch food, frogs rely mostly on their long, sticky tongues. Their tongues are much softer than your tongue, and as sticky as a warm marshmallow or chewing gum. Instead of attaching at the back, like your tongue does, an anuran's tongue attaches to

Most anurans use their long, sticky tongues to catch food. *MZPHOTO.CZ/Shutterstock.com*

45

Hunt Like an Amphibian

Walk around your yard or a park and look for foods that amphibians might eat: insects, spiders, minnows, and so on.

Try to think like an amphibian! Check (carefully) under logs and rocks, look on leaves and branches, and follow insects in flight. But instead of slurping up your discoveries with your tongue, take a photo or draw a picture instead.

Make a list in your explorer's notebook of all the amphibian delicacies you find, and include drawings or photos. If an amphibian lived in your neighborhood, would it be well fed? Or would it go hungry? Why do you think this is?

A kingfisher makes a meal of a tadpole. Many animals prey on amphibians. *Pierre Dalous/Wikimedia Commons*

crocodiles, turtles, raccoons, and other amphibians.

All living things are linked in complex food webs. Amphibians are an important part of many food webs. Without this food source, some predators might not survive. Some snakes, for example, only eat certain species of toads; if the toads disappear, the snakes will die out too.

HOW DO FROGS HELP HUMANS?

Frogs don't seem like they'd be all that helpful to humans. Some think their slimy or warty skin is icky, and most of us don't eat them. But a world without amphibians would be a lot itchier, more irritating, and much more dangerous, mostly because of what they eat.

Amphibians gobble pesky insects by the thousands. Without them, we'd be over-run with flies and mosquitoes, some of which can carry deadly human diseases.

Write a Slimy Story

MATERIALS

- Explorer's notebook
- Pen or pencil

In your explorer's notebook, write a story based on the pictures shown below, or choose your own amphibian subject. Be as realistic or as imaginative as you like.

Name your characters and choose a setting for your story. What problem does your character have? How will he or she solve it? This solution will be more satisfying if the character makes a couple of unsuccessful attempts to solve their problem before they finally succeed. Writers call this the "rule of three."

Edit your story to polish it, and add illustrations if you like. Then share it with a parent, teacher, or friend.

Alexas_Fotos/Pixabay

guentherlig/Pixabay

6

The Life Cycle

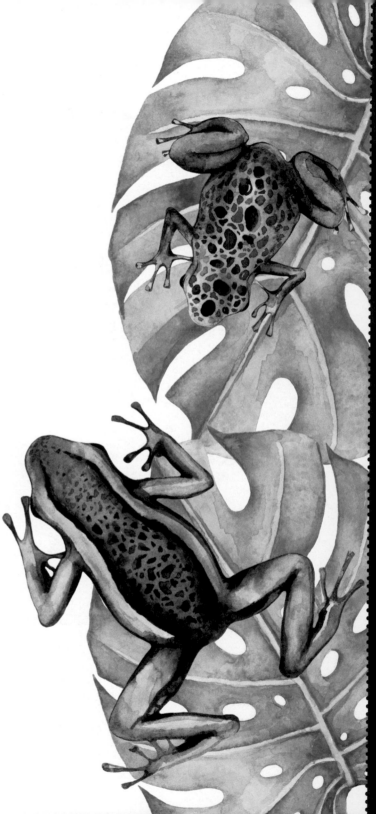

When you were born, you looked more or less like you do now—only smaller and with no teeth. Humans are not alone in this—most vertebrates are born looking like miniature versions of their parents.

Amphibians, however, break the mold. Many of them undergo dramatic changes in form as they develop. Anurans make the most extreme changes as they develop from egg to tadpole to frog. They eat different things and live in different places during each life stage. In fact, the body of a tadpole looks more like a fish than an adult frog. Salamanders and caecilians also change form as they grow, but not as dramatically.

Turn the page to see how it happens.

Skitterphoto/Pixabay

51

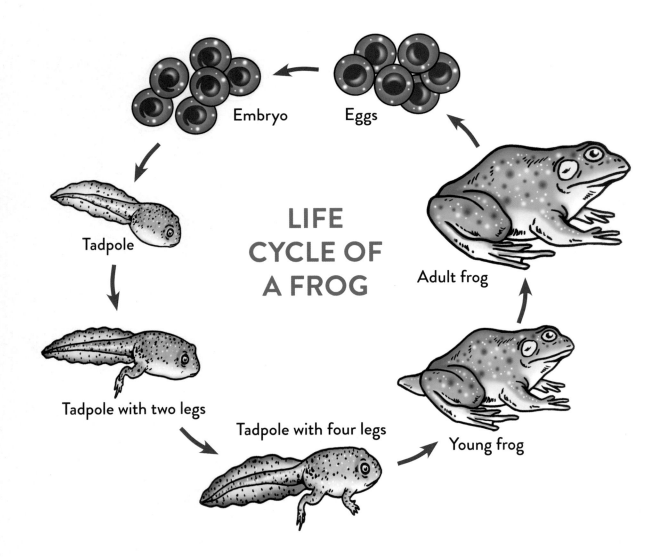

LIFE CYCLE OF A FROG

Eggs

Embryo

Tadpole

Tadpole with two legs

Tadpole with four legs

Young frog

Adult frog

Anurans undergo dramatic changes in form called metamorphosis.

Love Is in the Air

Humans have long used love songs to express their feelings. Perhaps they got the idea from frogs, which have been in the love song business for eons.

On spring nights, male frogs and toads sing loud mating songs in a quest to attract females. They space themselves out within their habitat and call loudly in a chorus. Each defends his own space and tries to outdo his neighbor's call. Some sing so loudly they can be heard a mile away.

Other male frogs also show off for females by spreading out their toes in a behavior called **semaphore,** or foot-flagging.

In cooler climates, frogs and toads can only breed when the temperature and rainfall are just right—not too cold, not too hot, and not too dry. So they tend to breed all at once in the spring. In the warm, humid tropics, anurans may breed anytime throughout the year.

With so many males competing for their attention, female frogs can afford to be choosy. They watch to see which mate is the biggest, most colorful, or strongest. They seem to prefer males that make longer, faster calls; perhaps these males are healthier and more energetic than others.

Eventually, each female will choose her mate, and the pair will head off to a good egg-laying site. The male is usually smaller than the female. He climbs onto her back and holds onto her waist. He then fertilizes the eggs with his sperm as they are laid. This mating behavior is called **amplexus**.

Salamander Dance

Since they cannot call as frogs do, salamanders use odors and elaborate dances to communicate with potential mates. In some species, the pair taps their chins together to transfer chemicals called pheromones. Then they perform a special walk, with the male straddling the female's tail.

In other species, the male waves his foot in an elaborate pattern. The male seepage salamander (*Desmognathus aeneus*) of the southeastern United States actually bites the female for a while.

After it has chosen a mate, a male salamander places a packet of sperm on the ground. The female picks it up with an opening in her body called the cloaca, and the sperm fertilize the eggs inside her body. The female will later lay a mass of eggs.

It Starts with an Egg

All amphibians start off as eggs. A few species carry their eggs inside until they hatch, but most lay them in or near water. These eggs don't look anything like the hard-shelled chicken eggs you might have eaten for breakfast. Instead, they are soft and squishy, like jelly. Inside each clear egg is a yolk, similar to the yellow yolk in a chicken egg. In amphibian eggs, however, the yolk is spread throughout the egg. The young feed on this yolk until they hatch.

(*left*) This dancing frog from India tries to attract a mate by spreading his toes wide. This behavior is known as foot-flagging. *SathyabhamaDasBiju/Wikimedia Commons*

(*right*) This pair of frogs is in amplexus. The much smaller male is on top. *Davidvraju/ Wikimedia Commons*

The Sierra newt throws back its head and tail when it is threatened. *Gary Nafis*

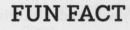

FUN FACT

How long do frogs live? It's difficult to know for sure. But some species have been known to live for up to 30 years in captivity.

known as the pebble toad because its color makes it look like a rock.

Fighting Back

Most amphibians are not aggressive, but some will fight back when they are attacked. In one study, scientists found that black-bellied salamanders snapped their teeth and then bit back when a shrew or hedgehog attacked them. The Sierra newt thrusts its head and tail into the air to make itself look more intimidating and to show off its brightly colored belly. Spadefoot toads give off a foul odor when they feel threatened.

Other amphibians puff themselves up to look scarier. This has the added bonus of making them harder for a snake or other predator to swallow. However, some predators have ways to deal with this problem. For example, the hognose snake has special fangs in the rear of its mouth to pop puffed-up toads.

Spiny newts such as the Spanish ribbed newt take the art of defense to a whole new level. Scientists at the University of Vienna discovered that when the Spanish ribbed newt is threatened, it secretes a toxin, then rotates its ribs and pushes them right through a set of warts on its skin to form spines. Each time the newt defends itself in

this way, it must poke a new set of holes in its skin.

Look Over There!

Some salamanders can lose their tails when they are threatened by a predator. This type of defense is known as misdirection. The salamander waves its tail to get the predator's attention, then detaches the tail from its body. *Zip!* The piece of tail left behind keeps wiggling and distracts the predator while the animal escapes. The salamander can grow a new tail to replace one that is lost. However, it takes a lot of energy to regrow a tail, so it is best for the animal to avoid losing its tail unless it is necessary.

When a salamander loses its tail, skin cells at the wound site quickly move around to cover it. Other cells called fibroblasts gather beneath the skin cells and develop into a mass called a blastema. The animal's genes tell the blastema which kind of body part it should develop into. This usually works well, but occasionally something goes wrong and the salamander ends up with a crooked tail or a double tail.

Playing Dead

The leaf litter frogs of Brazil play dead when threatened. These little frogs flop on their backs, throw out their limbs dramatically, and close their eyes. They can remain in this position for two minutes as they wait for the threat to leave.

The fire-bellied toads of Asia and Europe also flip over when threatened. This exposes their bright red bellies, warning predators that their skin is toxic.

When threatened, the fire-bellied toad flips onto its back to play dead. Its brightly colored belly warns predators to stay away. *Eric Isselee/ Shutterstock.com*

Creatures of the Night

Since amphibians prefer the damp, cool, nighttime air, many hunt only at night. This also makes them harder for predators to spot and lets them avoid predators such as birds that are not active at night. Being nocturnal helps these amphibians stay safe.

Hunting at night may not be as big of a challenge for amphibians as you might think. In a 2017 study, Swedish scientists found that frogs and toads can see color even in the dark. They use this ability not only to find their way around, but also to find food.

PLAYING "POSSUM"

Amphibians aren't the only animals that fake their own deaths when threatened. Many other animals try this trick as well. This behavior is called **thanatosis.**

Perhaps the best known actor is the opossum, which flops over on its side and gives a very convincing performance. The Southern hognose snake brings this trick to another level—not only does it flip over, it also gives off chemicals that make it smell dead. Some fish, insects, and spiders also play dead when they are threatened.

Make Your Yard Toad-Friendly

Do you want to attract toads to your yard? Not only are they fun to watch, they will help you out by gobbling pests.

Here are a few tips for making your yard toad-friendly.

1. Don't spray toxic chemicals around your house or yard. Pesticides, fertilizers, and herbicides can harm toads.

2. Put out a dish of water for toads to drink. Since toads also absorb water through their skin, make sure the toad can hop into it easily. A clay or plastic saucer is a good choice. Rinse and refill the dish at least once per week.

3. Provide a shelter for the toad to hide under. A flowerpot works well. Set a rock or two under the edge to prop it up, or cut a hole for a door.

4. Set up a toad light—a light no more than 3 feet (1 m) above the ground. This will attract night-flying insects, which toads like to eat.

8

A Dangerous World

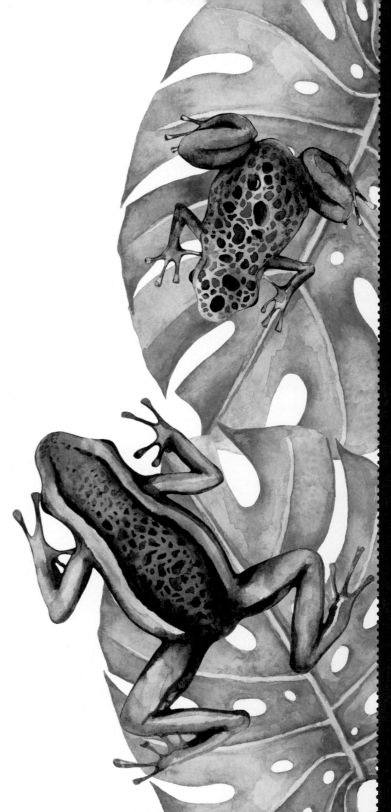

It's a tough time to be an amphibian. According to the International Union for the Conservation of Nature (IUCN), nearly a third of amphibian species are critically endangered, endangered, or vulnerable. Another quarter of them cannot be classified because there is not enough information about them.

Amphibians are going extinct 200 times faster than at any other time in history. Most of these extinctions are the result of human activities, either directly or indirectly. Often more than one factor is involved.

Shrinking Habitat

Imagine that one day your house started shrinking. First your bedroom would disappear, then your bathroom and kitchen. Eventually, you would have to move to a new house.

That is exactly what is happening to amphibians. Their habitats—their homes—are shrinking because of human activities. But because it is happening in so many places, and because they can't travel very far, amphibians can't always find another place to live.

Habitat loss is especially hard on amphibians because many of them live in two different habitats during their life cycle—in water and on land. While this can help animals by allowing them to use different resources, it also means that if either of their habitats is destroyed, they cannot survive. Living in two different habitats also means that they are twice as likely to be exposed to something that can harm them.

The human population passed 7 billion in 2011 and continues to grow. As the population grows, people cut down more forests, drain more wetlands, and build more homes, farms, and cities to meet their needs. All of these activities affect places where amphibians live and breed.

In tropical regions, rain forests are rapidly being cleared, swamps drained, rivers dammed, and waterways heated as they are used to cool nuclear power plants. More than 80 percent of all amphibian species live in these tropical forests. Some live in an extremely small area.

For instance, the Kihansi spray toad once lived only in the spray zone along the Kihansi River Gorge. When a hydroelectric dam was built in 2005, greatly reducing the volume of spray, the toads began to disappear. A sprinkler system was set up to try to save them, but system failures caused the ecosystem to dry up. Pesticides flushed through the dam may have also weakened the toads. Chytrid disease killed the few animals that were left, and by 2005, the species was extinct in the wild. Researchers at the Toledo and Bronx Zoos have been breeding the toads and reintroducing them into the area. They hope the new toads will be able to survive and reproduce.

Road Construction Ahead!

Roads can be a big problem for amphibians as well, especially large, busy highways that are difficult for the animals to cross.

A forest in Panama is destroyed by a process called slash-and-burn. *Dirk van der Made/Flickr*

(*left*) This tunnel in Germany allows amphibians to pass safely under the road. *Tegethof/Wikimedia Commons*

(*right*) This Limosa harlequin frog died of a fungal disease known as Bd, or chytrid disease. *Brian Gratwicke/ Flickr*

Roads also shrink amphibian habitats by cutting them up into smaller and smaller pieces. This is known as habitat **fragmentation**. When this happens, amphibians cannot move around as easily to find food and mates. In several US states and parts of Europe, people are building tunnels under roads to allow amphibians to cross safely when migrating. For some species, these tunnels can be lifesavers.

Not only does road construction destroy habitat, but the runoff from roads can cause pollution as well. Road crews sometimes apply deicing chemicals or salt to keep roads from freezing, and vehicles drip oil and gas onto the road. When it rains, these chemicals wash off into ditches and are carried into waterways.

A Froggy Fungus

In the late 1990s, scientists began to notice that something was killing amphibians worldwide. Frogs had started dying off in large numbers in the 1970s, but it took scientists decades to connect the dots. After some detective work, they traced the mystery disease to a type of fungus known as *Batrachochytrium dendrobatidis*, or Bd for short. It is sometimes referred to as chytridiomycosis, amphibian chytrid, or chytrid (pronounced KIT-trid) disease.

Chytrid disease spreads via free-swimming cells called **zoospores**. When a zoospore lands on an amphibian's skin, it digs into a cell and produces a **thallus** that releases 40 to 100 more zoospores. Since amphibians breathe through their skin, these growths affect their oxygen levels, and the balance of electrolytes in their blood gets messed up. Eventually an animal with chytrid disease has a heart attack and dies.

Scientists believe the disease started in the Korean peninsula in the 1950s. It probably spread through human activity such as the Korean War, the meat and pet industries, and the shipping of frogs for use in pregnancy tests.

Today, people move goods and animals around the world at a faster rate than ever before. As a result, diseases spread more rapidly as well—including chytrid disease. The fungus can also travel on the clothes and shoes of humans, even the researchers who are studying it, if they are not careful. So it is very important to disinfect field gear before and after hiking.

Another likely factor in the spread of chytrid disease is stress. The stresses caused by other factors such as a changing climate and polluted waters may weaken amphibians. This makes them more likely to get sick when they are exposed to the fungus. Strong, healthy animals can more easily fight off disease.

A Medical Mystery

Since the 1950s, scientists have been trying to solve a mystery: why are so many frogs with extra legs, missing legs, or twisted legs turning up in the United States and Canada? These deformities are happening at a much higher rate than ever before. In some places, as many as 4 out of every 10 frogs are deformed. Scientists believe there are three possible explanations for this problem: predators, parasites, and pollution.

Predators

In some cases, missing frog legs can be traced to a natural culprit: dragonfly nymphs. These young insects live at the bottom of streams and lakes. They are not large enough to eat a whole tadpole. But they can bite off a leg with their razor-sharp jaws. The missing leg may become deformed, or may not grow back at all. However, this is a natural process, so it cannot explain the large number of deformities in some areas.

Parasites

Certain kinds of flatworms can be transferred to amphibians through bird feces. An intermediate stage of these parasites infects pond snails. The parasite is then released into ponds and swims around until it burrows into the body of a tadpole, close to the place where its legs normally grow. This can cause the tadpole to grow deformed legs or even extra legs.

Scientists say that pesticides and fertilizers found in farm runoff can increase the numbers of these parasites. The chemicals cause more algae to grow, which means more food for the pond snail hosts. As snail numbers increase, so does the number of parasites.

Pollutants

Imagine that you are sitting in a bathtub when someone pours in a bucket of dirt or a dangerous chemical. You would leap out as soon as you could! But amphibians don't

This frog developed an extra set of legs after being infected by a parasite.
Pieter Johnson/Oregon State University/Flickr

74

have that option. A tadpole or salamander larva is stuck living in its pond or stream no matter how polluted it becomes. And because amphibians' skin is so thin and permeable, pesticides and other pollutants can easily soak into their bodies.

Pesticides, fertilizers, heavy metals, road salt, and pollutants released from mining or logging can wash off into amphibian breeding sites. These chemicals can either kill young amphibians or cause them to develop abnormally. Even if they live on land, adult amphibians are affected by pollution when they eat contaminated insects and other small animals.

Amphibians affected by these chemicals may grow deformed limbs or may not be able to reproduce normally. One particular chemical known as atrazine is widely used to kill weeds in farm crops. Atrazine has been found to affect the development of male frogs, making them look more like females. This chemical can also change the sex of some fish from male to female.

Acid Rain

Have you ever tasted vinegar? Or a lemon? These foods have a sharp, tart taste because they contain acids. Your stomach also contains acids that help break down foods.

 TRY THIS!

How Thin Is Frog Skin?

An amphibian's thin skin is permeable—that is, it lets molecules of water, oxygen, and other gases pass through easily. To see how this works, try this experiment with a chicken egg, which has a semipermeable membrane under its shell. You'll use vinegar (acetic acid) to remove the shell. Then you'll be left with a "naked egg" surrounded only by the membrane.

MATERIALS

- Egg
- Food coloring (any color)
- Disposable plastic cup
- Vinegar

1. Place an egg in a disposable cup and cover it with vinegar.

2. Add several drops of food coloring to the cup.

3. Let the egg sit, undisturbed, for 24 hours.

4. Gently pour off the vinegar and rinse the egg with water. Add fresh vinegar and food coloring, as above.

5. Let the egg sit for another 24 hours.

6. Carefully remove the egg. Handle with care! The shell should have dissolved, so the egg will feel soft and squishy. If the shell has not completely dissolved, repeat steps 4 and 5.

7. Cut open the egg over a bowl. Did the dye pass through the membrane?

Making Acid Rain

Acid rain forms as a result of air pollution. In this activity, you'll use an acid you can probably find in your pantry—vinegar—to learn how acid can affect objects that it comes in contact with. Vinegar is made up of acetic acid and is a relatively mild acid.

MATERIALS

- 1 cup vinegar
- 1 cup distilled water
- 2 eggshells
- 2 leaves
- 2 dirty coins
- 2 glass jars
- Explorer's notebook

1. Put a cup of vinegar into one jar. Put a cup of distilled water into the other.

2. Place one eggshell, leaf, and coin into each jar.

3. Allow the items to soak overnight.

4. What do you think will happen to the items? Write down your predictions in your explorer's notebook.

5. The following day, examine each object and note its condition in your notebook. Return each to the jar.

6. Let the jars sit for six more days, then look at the objects again.

7. Write down your observations in your explorer's notebook. What happened to each item? If the outcome did not match your prediction, can you think of a reason for that? What do you think would happen to an amphibian or its eggs if acid were poured into its aquatic habitat?

THE OZONE LAYER

High above the Earth lies a layer of gas called ozone. Ozone is a special type of oxygen. This layer helps block harmful rays from the sun known as ultraviolet B (UV-B) radiation. However, because of pollutants called chlorofluorocarbons (CFCs) that were put into the atmosphere over a period of 50 years, the ozone layer has shrunk by about 20 percent in some areas. As a result, more UV-B is now reaching the Earth.

Ultraviolet B radiation can cause skin cancer in humans and also affects amphibian eggs and young. It can slow their growth and cause deformities and even death.

The United States and some European countries banned the use of some chemicals found to be harmful to the ozone layer by 1996. The ozone layer is slowly recovering, but it will take many years to return to its original thickness.

cloud base around the forest is rising higher into the air. As a result, the air in the forest is getting drier.

In some amphibians, the sex of the eggs is determined by the temperature of the environment. So changes in temperature can cause there to be too many males or too many females.

Scientists are already recording changes in the **phenology**, or seasonal cycles, of amphibians. Spring peepers in New York, for example, now start calling 11 to 14 days earlier than they did a century ago. Ornate chorus frogs in California are breeding up to eight weeks later than they used to.

(*left*) Climate change is causing mists to rise in the Monteverde Cloud Forest, making the environment drier. *Juhku/Shutterstock.com*

will never be cuddly like cats and dogs. And they must be kept at just the right temperature and humidity to survive. You'll need to purchase insects or baby mice to feed your amphibian, depending on the species.

Laws limit which species can be collected from the wild. So if you buy a pet, it's important to make sure it was not illegally collected. Buying from a breeder with a good reputation is the best way to make sure your pet is legal.

If you do decide to keep an amphibian as a pet, make sure to wash your hands before and after handling it, and never touch your eyes, nose, or mouth while you're handling it. Unless you have your own well, make sure not to give it water straight from the tap. The chlorine in city water supplies can hurt or even kill amphibians. You'll need a water conditioner to remove the chlorine from the water.

Keep the animal's home clean to prevent disease, and remember that amphibians can live for years. If you get tired of your pet, you need to find a responsible person to take care of it. ***Never* release a pet into the wild.** Pets released into the wild can carry disease and can also become invasive.

DO TOADS CAUSE WARTS?

Many people believe that handling a toad can cause warts. This is simply not true. A toad's warts are made of a material called keratin, just like the material in your fingernails and hair. Human warts, on the other hand, are areas of thickened skin caused by a virus called HPV, which is contagious. It can be spread by sharing towels, utensils, or other objects with a person who has warts. So you won't catch warts from a toad—but you might catch them from a human!

Laws Protecting Amphibians

Laws vary from country to country, and even from state to state within the United States. But many countries now have laws to protect endangered amphibians.

In the United States, the most important of these laws is the Endangered Species Act of 1973. This law gives government agencies the power to protect endangered species and their habitat. For example, anyone who wants to destroy a pond where one of these species lives must first replace it so that the animals can be moved.

Another important US law is the Lacey Act of 1900, which was updated in 2008. It bans anyone from importing any plants or animals, including amphibians, that are considered dangerous to human health, agriculture, forestry, or wildlife. This law is designed to keep invasive species from entering the country and becoming a problem.

9

~~~~~~

Working with Amphibians

Scientists study amphibians for many different reasons. Some hope to find new medical procedures and drugs. Others are working to conserve and protect endangered species of amphibians. Still others study how amphibians are related to each other and search for new species that have not yet been identified. If you love studying amphibians, you might want to consider one of these careers!

A researcher examines a frog in the laboratory. *Brian Gratwicke/Flickr*

Search for a Cure

Frogs have been important in scientific research since at least 1487, when Leonardo da Vinci discovered that a frog's brain controls its other organs. In the 1700s, Italian scientist Luigi Galvani's study of frogs showed that electricity was involved in the nervous system. In the 1950s, the first successful cloning technique was performed on a frog.

Today, scientists are trying to learn how frogs can help cure diseases and injuries. Even highly toxic frogs can be useful in medicine. The phantasmal poison frog of Ecuador secretes a highly toxic poison that is also, in tiny amounts, quite good at relieving pain. It is too dangerous to use on humans, but scientists have created a similar compound in the lab that safely mimics its effects. The drug is still being tested but shows promise to one day replace the more addictive painkillers commonly used today.

Scientists have known for some time that chemicals in frog skin have some disease-killing powers. In a recent study, researchers at Vanderbilt University found that compounds in the skin of the Australian red-eyed tree frog can also destroy human immunodeficiency virus (HIV), the virus that causes a disease called AIDS. They hope that these compounds may someday lead to a cure for this disease.

Another area of medical research focuses on salamanders. Scientists are interested in learning how some species can regrow their tails, limbs, and parts of their jaw. Perhaps someday these discoveries will be used to help people regrow organs, limbs, or other tissues after severe injuries.

Saving Amphibians

Scientists around the world are working to study and catalog the world's amphibian species and to find ways to protect them. Happily, in recent years, scientists have rediscovered some species that were once thought to be extinct.

In 2010, scientists from Conservation International and the IUCN's Amphibian Specialist Group searched 21 countries for amphibian species that had not been seen for at least 10 years and were thought to be extinct. They rediscovered 13 species of frogs and one species of salamander, although many others were never found. In 2017, biologists rediscovered the Jackson's climbing salamander in Guatemala. This beautiful yellow-and-black salamander had not been seen for 30 years.

 **TRY THIS!**

Write an Amphibian Haiku

Haiku is an ancient Japanese form of poetry that is still popular today. Haiku poems follow a set pattern. They are three lines long. The first line has five syllables, the second has seven syllables, and the third has five syllables. The lines do not need to rhyme; in fact, most do not.

These poems traditionally mention an element of nature, so amphibians make a great subject. Try writing your own amphibian haiku and share it with a friend or family member! Here's an example to get you started.

Frogs call in moonlight.
Ribbet! Ribbet! Look at me!
Croaking, leaping. Splash!

GERM KILLERS

Until the mid-1900s, African clawed frogs were used to test whether women were pregnant. If a sample of her urine injected into the frog's leg caused the frog to start laying eggs, doctors knew the woman was pregnant.

While raising frogs for these tests, some scientists noticed that the frogs' wounds healed quickly, even in dirty water. They wondered if some mystery chemical was killing the germs. They decided to investigate. They were right! Chemicals called peptides in the frogs' skin turned out to be very good at killing fungi, parasites, and viruses.

Other scientists are working at bringing species back, a process known as de-extinction. For example, a team led by Michael Archer at the University of New South Wales, University of Newcastle, took cell nuclei from tissues of an extinct frog that had been frozen in the 1970s. They inserted them into eggs of a great barred frog and were able to get the DNA to replicate. They have not yet been able to re-create the frog, but they are well on their way. Perhaps one day, this technology will be used to bring other extinct species back to life as well.

Fighting the Fungus

Because chytrid disease is killing so many amphibians worldwide, scientists are looking for a cure. Many possible treatments have been studied.

Studies show that a medication used to treat athlete's foot in humans can cure amphibians infected with the disease. However, so far there is no good way to apply it to frogs in the wild. And while it can cure an individual animal, it is impossible to remove the fungus from the environment. If an affected animal is treated

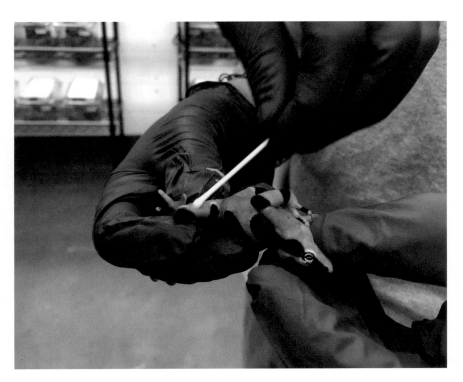

Researchers swab a golden frog to test for chytrid disease. *Brian Gratwicke/Flickr*

and released, it may be re-infected with the disease.

Researchers at the San Francisco Zoo and Oakland Zoo are experimenting with immunizing frogs against the fungus. Just as your doctor gives you shots to protect you against diseases like chicken pox, the scientists expose the frogs to a small amount of fungus in the lab. This may help the frogs' immune systems fight off the fungus when they are released into the wild.

Other methods are being studied as well. A team of scientists from Spain and the United Kingdom successfully cured a whole population of midwife toads by disinfecting their breeding habitats with an industrial cleaner. Still another group at Virginia Tech is looking at using "good" bacteria to help frogs fight the disease. But some people wonder if it is a good idea to release new bacteria into an environment where they do not naturally occur.

At the Zoo

Zoos are fun places to visit and learn about animals. They help teach people about wild animals and how to protect them. They also play an important role in breeding endangered species to release into the wild.

Write to an Amphibian Scientist

With a parent or teacher's help, find the name of an amphibian scientist. Learn about their organization and what they do. The organization's website is a good place to start.

Make a list of questions you would like to ask the scientist, and write an e-mail or letter thanking them for their work and asking your questions. You may want to ask how you can help.

If they write back, share the letter with your friends or classmates.

A biologist at the Saratoga National Fish Hatchery feeds live worms to endangered Wyoming toads. The Wyoming toad is extinct in the wild. Several organizations are working to save the species so it can one day return to the wild. *USFWS Mountain-Prairie/Wikimedia Commons*

One of these species is the endangered Wyoming toad. The Detroit Zoo is one of several organizations working to reintroduce this species into the wild. More than 8,000 juvenile and adult toads have been released since 1995.

In January 2018, researchers released about 500 variable harlequin frogs in Panama in preparation for a larger release later on. These frogs are endangered due to chytrid disease. The Panama Amphibian Rescue and Conservation project (PARC) at the Smithsonian Conservation Biology Institute has been breeding the frogs at several zoos in order to keep the species alive. When they were released, the frogs were tagged with radio transmitters so the scientists will be able to track them and learn what happens to them.

Studying Amphibians

Amphibians can be hard to find, which makes them hard to study. So, some scientists use traps to catch them. One technique is to use a sheet of aluminum or fencing to create a "drift fence" near a wetland. Buckets or funnel traps are placed in the ground

(*left*) Two researchers survey frog populations in Panama. *Brian Gratwicke/Flickr*

(*right*) Fluorescent tags in this frog's legs will allow scientists to identify it when they recapture it in the wild. That way they can monitor the population. *Brian Gratwicke/Flickr*

along the fence. Amphibians can't hop over the fence, so they move along the edge of it searching for an entrance and fall into one of the traps.

Frog populations can also be studied by simply listening to their calls. Volunteers record the time, location, and number of calls they hear during the breeding season. These records can be compared from year to year to track populations. One long-term program was run by the US Geological Survey at the Patuxent Wildlife Research Center in Maryland. It monitored frog and toad calls from 1994 to 2015.

A more high-tech method of recording frog calls is by using "frogloggers." These recording devices can be placed near wetlands to record the calls. The recordings can reveal the time of day that frogs typically call, their response to airplane noise, and other interesting information.

Yet another way to study amphibians is to examine or count their eggs. Egg masses are easier to find than adult amphibians, and a few can usually be removed for testing without harming the rest. Only experienced scientists should do this, though.

Sometimes, it's important for scientists to examine individual frogs. In order to track individual animals, scientists may do a capture-mark-recapture study. They capture the animal, measure and examine it, mark it, and then release it. Later, if the animal is recaptured, it will be again measured and examined. Different methods are used to mark amphibians, including clipping a toe, injecting a fluorescent dye or tag under the skin, or inserting a microchip that will transmit a signal back to a chip reader. Sometimes scientists dust the animal with

Draw a Frog

Try drawing this cute little frog. Then give him a lily pad to sit on and a fly to eat. Fill in the scenery around him—a pond, some trees, and whatever else you'd like to add.

MATERIALS

- Explorer's notebook
- Pencil
- Black marker
- Markers, crayons, or colored pencils

1. Draw an oval for the head.

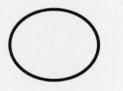

2. Add two circles for eyes and an oval for the belly. Fill in eyeballs, and add a nose and mouth.

3. Draw the frog's legs.

4. Add four webbed feet.

5. Outline your frog with black marker. Then color it in with a marker, crayon, or colored pencil.

fluorescent powder so they can follow its trail and see where it goes.

The best information can be collected using radio transmitters, but these can be difficult to attach and are more expensive to use than other methods.

Working Together

Many organizations are working to protect amphibians and their habitats from further catastrophe. There is not space to list them all here, but here are a few well-known examples.

Amphibian Ark is a joint effort of three organizations: the World Association of Zoos and Aquariums (WAZA), the IUCN SSC Conservation Planning Specialist Group (CPSG), and the Amphibian Specialist Group (ASG). Amphibian Ark is working to protect species that cannot be protected in their natural habitat by breeding them in captivity. They are trying to keep the animals from going extinct so hopefully they can one day return to the wild.

Save the Frogs works to educate people about the dangers that amphibians face and help protect their habitat. The organization also works with lawmakers to protect wetland areas and to do research to help prevent species from going extinct.

The Amphibian Survival Alliance is dedicated to amphibian conservation, research, and education. The group works with governments, industries, nonprofits, and individuals to protect habitats and research diseases as well as to help people understand the threats that amphibians face.

10

How You Can Help

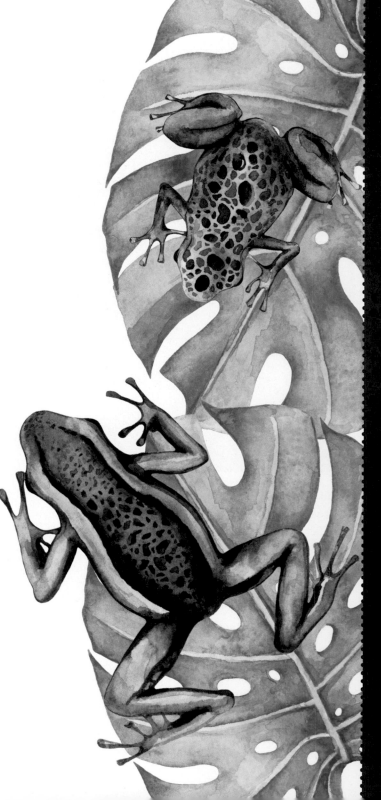

Tackling big problems can be discouraging. How can any one of us fight such a huge problem as climate change or pollution? How can we save a rain forest from clearcutting?

We can't—on our own. But as anthropologist Margaret Mead once said, "Never doubt that a small group of thoughtful, committed citizens can change the world. Indeed, it is the only thing that ever has." One of us may not be able to do everything, but all of us can do something.

In this chapter, you will find some ways that you and your friends can get involved and help to protect amphibians.

If you pick up an amphibian, handle it gently. After you've looked at it, place it gently back into its habitat. *Steve Hillebrand, US Fish and Wildlife Service/Wikimedia Commons*

Share What You Know

One way you can help make a difference for amphibians is to share what you know. Tell your parents and your friends about the dangers that amphibians face. Ask your teacher if you can share information with your class. The more people know, the more they can help, and the more they will want to help. You might also want to write a letter to the editor of your school or local newspaper to encourage people to get involved.

Earth Day is another good opportunity to share information about amphibian conservation. This holiday is celebrated on April 22 every year. It marks the anniversary of the beginning of the environmental movement in 1970. Many communities and schools plan Earth Day events to help raise awareness of environmental issues and encourage people to help protect the Earth. Perhaps you could make a poster or display about amphibians to share at an Earth Day event.

Another way to share your message is to write letters to your government officials to encourage them to make a difference. Ask them for stronger laws to protect wetland areas and other amphibian habitats. Urge them to protect endangered species as well. Few people take the time to write to their legislators, so your letters really can make a difference. And when you get old enough, you can vote.

LOBBYING LAWMAKERS

Students at Grizzell Middle School in Columbus, Ohio, learned firsthand how lobbying lawmakers can make a difference.

Beginning in 2002, students in teacher Shawn Kaeser's class wrote letters to their state senator, asking her to introduce a bill to recognize the bullfrog as the state amphibian. When a Cleveland-area school argued in 2009 that the spotted salamander should be the state amphibian instead, a compromise was reached. In 2010, the bullfrog was designated the state frog and the salamander the state amphibian.

Put Up a Poster

The more people know about an issue, the more they care. Many scientists make posters to present their research to others. You can make a poster to share what you've learned about an endangered amphibian. Include some simple actions that people can take to protect it. Help spread the word!

MATERIALS

- Books or websites about amphibians
- Poster board
- Markers
- Glue

1. Research endangered amphibians. The IUCN Red List and Amphibian Ark websites are good places to start.

2. Select an amphibian to focus on. Draw or print photos of your animal.

3. Write or type up a description of your animal, including interesting facts about the species.

4. Make a list of challenges that your amphibian faces. These might include logging, habitat loss, pollutants, hunting, etc.

5. Draw or print a map of the animal's habitat.

6. Make a list of actions people can take to help protect this animal.

7. Glue all of these items onto a piece of poster board. Add a colorful title and decorate your poster with markers.

8. Display your poster in your classroom or in another public place.

Just Eat It!

One growing solution to the problem of invasive species is to eat them! While hunting native amphibians can harm populations, the opposite is true for invaders. Hunting invaders is a simple, nontoxic way to remove them from the ecosystem. This can help native populations to recover.

Invasive fish, weeds, birds, insects, amphibians, and even rodents have been turning up on the menu in restaurants across the United States. Of course, it's important to make sure the species is safe to eat first—you don't want to eat a poisonous cane toad! American bullfrogs, for example, can be served up as frog legs. And eating the invasive red swamp crayfish can help protect the tadpoles it preys on.

Get Your Hands Dirty!

Another way you can help is to join a school group or community group that is working to clean up and protect wetlands. Check with your city's park district or nature centers for ideas. Many states have chapters of the Sierra Club, the Audubon Society, or other conservation groups. Many states also have herpetological societies that offer meetings and programs where

WHAT'S YOUR STATE AMPHIBIAN?

Did you know that 23 states and Puerto Rico have an official state amphibian? Ohio and North Carolina even have two—a state frog and a state salamander. Can you find your state on the list? If it doesn't have a state amphibian, consider writing to your state representative to suggest one.

Alabama	Red Hills salamander	New Hampshire	Red-spotted newt
Arizona	Arizona tree frog	New Mexico	New Mexico spadefoot toad
California	California red-legged frog	New York	Wood frog
Colorado	Western tiger salamander	North Carolina	Pine barrens tree frog, Marbled salamander
Georgia	American green tree frog	Ohio	Spotted salamander, American bullfrog
Idaho	Idaho giant salamander	Oklahoma	American bullfrog
Illinois	Eastern tiger salamander	Puerto Rico	Common coqui
Iowa	American bullfrog	South Carolina	Spotted salamander
Kansas	Barred tiger salamander	Tennessee	Tennessee cave salamander
Louisiana	American green tree frog	Texas	Texas toad
Minnesota	Northern leopard frog	Vermont	Northern leopard frog
Missouri	American bullfrog	Washington	Pacific tree frog

you can go out with a group of experts and look for amphibians close to home.

Other groups to check out are the Children & Nature Network, Kids for Saving Earth, Earth Rangers, and Earth Force. These groups may do cleanup activities, plant trees, or lead hikes that you can join. You may even be able to help with raising money to help protect wildlife. If there's not a club near you, perhaps you can start your own.

An Amphibian-Friendly Habitat

Building new homes for amphibians can help them thrive. Ask your parents or school to consider building a garden pond. Studies show that newts, frogs, and toads quickly move into newly built ponds. Even small ponds can help, as long as they are not stocked with fish that might feed on amphibians or their eggs. And make sure not to introduce nonnative frogs that will compete with the species you are trying to help. Your new friends will repay you by gobbling up garden pests and mosquitoes.

A volunteer checks a bucket along an amphibian fence in Germany. *J.-H. Janßen/Wikimedia Commons*

Since amphibians are highly sensitive to chemicals, try not to use toxic sprays around your home. Chemicals that are commonly used to control weeds in yards, flowerbeds, or garden ponds can harm amphibians. Even chemicals used in your home can affect amphibians, as

Make a Toad Abode

Invite toads to move into your yard or garden with this adorable toad abode. Like most amphibians, toads like damp, cool places to live. This little house will give them shelter and keep them out of the sun's rays. Placing it near your garden will not only provide the toad a source of food, but will help you cut down on garden pests like slugs and insects. Set a little dish of water nearby to help attract your toad.

MATERIALS

- Clay flowerpot
- Craft materials: paints, mosaic tiles, glue, etc.
- Saucer
- Stones
- Trowel

1. Decorate a clay pot as desired using paints, tiles, glue, etc.

2. With the trowel, dig a hole in the soil about 4 inches (10 cm) deep and wide enough for the pot to lie in.

3. Lay the pot on its side. About half of the pot should be underground. Fill the underground part of the pot with soil to create a dirt floor.

4. Set a saucer of water nearby. Place some stones in the center if the water is deep.

5. You may want to make a welcome sign or other decorations for your toad abode.

WELCOME

they are difficult to remove in water treatment plants and can find their way into waterways.

Do you have a swimming pool in your yard or community? If you should happen to find frog eggs in the pool, carefully remove them and place them in fresh water. This is the one time you *do* want to disturb an animal's eggs. Otherwise, the chemicals in the pool will kill the eggs.

Become a Citizen Scientist

Did you know you don't have to be a trained scientist to help with scientific research? Citizen science projects let everyone help collect scientific information and protect the environment.

One of the first citizen science projects was the Audubon Society's Christmas Bird Count, which has been running for more than a hundred years. Other current projects track butterflies, invasive plants, horseshoe crabs, and even light pollution.

One citizen science project focused on amphibians is FrogWatch USA. This program is run by the Association of Zoos & Aquariums. Thousands of FrogWatch volunteers collect data about frog calls on evenings from February through August. Then they upload them to an online database. Scientists can use this data to study frog populations over time and to learn how humans can better protect them. The FrogWatch USA program started in 1998. Today there are more than 140 chapters throughout the United States. If you'd like to volunteer, visit the FrogWatch USA website, www.aza.org/frogwatch, to learn how you can help.

Crossing Safely

As mentioned earlier, in early spring, many frogs and salamanders migrate to pools of water to breed. They often must cross busy roads to get there. As a result, many amphibians are killed by passing cars.

In some areas, groups of people watch for the migration to begin and come out at night to help these amphibians safely

"HOPPY" FROG MONTH!

Celebrate frogs with two annual holidays! April is National Frog Month. During this month, amphibians in northern climates are on the move. And Save the Frogs Day takes place on the last Saturday in April. Events are held in many countries around the world to celebrate this day.

Jee & Rani Nature Photography/Wikimedia Commons

Track Your Water Usage

Clean, fresh water is an increasingly scarce resource. As the human population grows, more and more water is needed to meet our needs. One way you can help amphibians is to conserve water. Here are a few ideas:

- Turn off the faucet while you brush your teeth
- Take short showers instead of baths

- Don't let water run while you wash dishes
- Turn off the water while you scrub your hands
- Reuse rinse water to water plants
- Drink water from the tap instead of bottled water; if your water tastes bad, try a pitcher with a filter.

- Collect rainwater and use it to water plants.

Track how much water you use by filling out the chart below each day for a week. Then add up the columns. To figure out how much you use per year, multiply your weekly total by 52.

Weekly Water Usage (USGS Figures)	Sunday	Monday	Tuesday	Wednesday	Thursday	Friday	Saturday
Washing hands (1 gallon)							
Flushing the toilet (3 gallons)							
Washing a load of laundry (25–40 gallons)							
Washing dishes by hand (8–27 gallons)							
Washing dishes in a dishwasher (6–16 gallons)							
Drinking water (8 ounces per glass)							
Bath (36 gallons)							
Shower (5 gallons per minute, older showers; 2 gallons per minute, low-flow shower heads)							
Brushing teeth (1 gallon)							
Daily Totals							

cross the road. In some places, stretches of road are closed until the migration is over. Check with your local nature center or park system to see if you and a parent can help.

Sometimes salamanders must cross roadways as they migrate to their breeding ponds. Volunteers can help direct traffic to keep them safe. *weidegruen/Flickr*

Glossary

adaptation A change in a species over time that allows it to better survive in its environment

amplexus The mating position of frogs

anuran A member of order Anura; a frog or toad

aposematic Having coloration or markings that warn predators to stay away

binomial nomenclature The system of giving two names to each type of organism—the genus and species

bioindicator An organism whose status is used to determine the health of an ecosystem as a whole

cannibalism The practice of eating other members of one's own species

carnivore An animal that eats meat

cartilage A firm but flexible material found in the ear, joints, larynx, and other parts of the body

chromatophore A cell that contains pigment

clutch A group of eggs laid at the same time

countershading A type of camouflage in which the top of an animal is darker than its underside

ectothermy The regulation of body temperature by the outside environment

endothermic Able to create heat internally

estivation A period of dormancy during a hot, dry period

feces Waste material produced by the body after food has been digested

fragmentation The process of being broken into small pieces

frogspawn Frog eggs

gills Organs used by some amphibians to breathe underwater

habitat The natural home of an organism

herbivore An animal that eats plants

hibernate To spend the winter in a dormant state

invasive species A species that is not native to a habitat and tends to spread and harm the ecosystem

invertebrate An animal without a backbone

keratin A protein that makes up hair, teeth, claws, etc.

keratinized Made up of a hard substance called keratin

kingdom The largest category used to classify animals

metamorphosis A change in form

native A species that naturally occurs in an area

nocturnal Active at night

oviduct A tube that an egg passes through in a female animal

permeable Allowing liquids or gases to pass through

phenology The study of seasonal natural cycles

pheromone A chemical produced by an animal that affects the behavior of others of its species

phylum The category of classification under a kingdom

prehensile Able to grasp

semaphore A method of sending messages by holding out body parts in a certain position

taxonomist A scientist who groups organisms into categories

temperate Having mild temperatures

thallus A mass of fungal cells

thanatosis The defensive behavior of faking death

torpor A state of inactivity

tympanum A membrane that allows an amphibian to hear

venomous Able to inject toxins through a bite or sting

vertebrate An animal with a backbone

zoospore A fungal spore that can swim using a taillike flagellum

Amphibian Orders

Amphibians belong to class Amphibia. They can be divided into three different orders: Anura (frogs and toads), Caudata (salamanders and newts), and Gymnophiona (caecilians). Each of these orders is subdivided into many different families. Below are a few common examples mentioned in this book.

ORDER	
Anura	Tree frogs
Anura	True frogs
Anura	Fleshbelly frogs
Anura	Narrow-mouthed frogs
Anura	True toads
Caudata	Sirens
Caudata	Mudpuppies
Caudata	Olms
Caudata	Amphiumas

ORDER	
Caudata	Newts
Caudata	Mole salamanders
Caudata	Lungless salamanders
Caudata	Giant salamanders
Gymnophiona	Buried-eyed caecilians
Gymnophiona	Tropical African caecilians
Gymnophiona	Common caecilians
Gymnophiona	South American caecilians

Resources

Many organizations offer information about amphibians as well as ways that students can get involved. Here are a few that you may want to start with. Check for local chapters of national organizations, nature centers, and state or national parks in your area for more possibilities.

Amphibian and Reptile Conservancy:
    https://amphibianandreptileconservancy.org

Amphibian Ark: http://www.amphibianark.org

Amphibian Specialist Group (ASG) and Amphibian Survival Alliance (ASA): http://www.amphibians.org

AmphibiaWeb: https://amphibiaweb.org

HerpNet: http://www.herpnet.org

IUCN Red List: http://www.iucnredlist.org

Nature Conservancy: www.nature.org

Partners in Amphibian and Reptile Conservation:
    http://parcplace.org

Save the Frogs! https://www.savethefrogs.com

Society for the Study of Amphibians and Reptiles:
    https://ssarherps.org

Chris Mattison/Nature Picture Library

Teacher's Guide

The activities and information in this book can be used with a wide range of ages, either in the classroom or for independent study. If you'd like to explore further, consider some of the ideas below.

- ❏ Create an amphibian word search or crossword puzzle.

- ❏ Ask students to research your state amphibian and create a presentation about it. Alternatively, have each student research a different species that lives in your area and share their findings with the class.

- ❏ Research any endangered species in your area and find out how your students can get involved in protecting them.

- ❏ Make amphibian conservation a focus of your Earth Day activities.

- ❏ Have students nominate and vote on a class amphibian. Research the winning species and have students draw it. Perhaps you will want to give your amphibian a fun name.

- ❏ Look around your neighborhood for amphibian habitats with your students.

- ❏ Take a field trip to a local nature center or park in spring to look for signs of amphibians and listen for frog calls.

- ❏ Brainstorm ways that your class can get involved with amphibian conservation activities.

- ❏ Ask your students to compare and contrast the following:
  - 🦎 Anurans, caecilians, and salamanders
  - 🦎 Frogs and toads
  - 🦎 Vertebrates and invertebrates
  - 🦎 Amphibians and reptiles

pirhan/Flickr

❑ Discuss the following questions:

🐸 Why do people tend to overlook or even dislike amphibians?

🐸 What important roles do amphibians play in the ecosystem?

🐸 How do amphibians help humans?

🐸 What do scientists mean when they talk about bioindicator species?

🐸 Why is it important to protect amphibians?

🐸 Do amphibians make good pets? Why or why not?

❑ Research one of these scientists further.

🐸 Carl Linnaeus

🐸 Leonardo da Vinci

🐸 Luigi Galvani

Bibliography

~~~~~~

Denotes titles suitable for young readers.

Ballard, Bonnie, and Ryan Cheek, eds. *Exotic Animal Medicine for the Veterinary Technician*. New York: John Wiley & Sons, 2016.

Dorcas, Mike, and Whit Gibbons. *Frogs: The Animal Answer Guide*. Baltimore, MD: The Johns Hopkins University Press, 2011.

*Green, David M., Linda A. Weird, Gary S. Casper, and Michael J. Lannoo. *North America Amphibians: Distribution & Diversity*. Berkeley: University of California Press, 2013.

Pough, F. Harvey, Robin M. Andrews, Martha L. Crump, Alan H. Savitzky, Kentwood D. Wells, and Matthew C. Brandley. *Herpetology, Fourth Edition*. Sunderland, MA: Sinauer Associates, 2016.

*Tkaczyk, Filip. *Tracks & Sign of Reptiles & Amphibians: A Guide to North American Species*. Mechanicsburg, PA: Stackpole Books, 2015.

Other Resources

Many other magazine articles, scientific journal articles, and online sources were also consulted during the writing of this book. These included AmphibiaWeb, Animal Diversity Web, National Geographic, the National Park Service, the World Association of Zoos and Aquariums, the San Diego Zoo, Smithsonian's National Zoo & Conservation Biology Institute, and the International Union for the Conservation of Nature (IUCN), among others.

Index